"This is one of the best Christian books I have read in the past five years. Matt Fuller has the courage to speak to a vital question and to do so with refreshing boldness, enviable clarity, loving warmth, and some delicious humour. His practical pastoral experience breathes through every chapter. Every man—and woman too—will benefit from reading it, and it will make a superb volume for a book group."

**CHRISTOPHER ASH,** Writer-in-Residence, Tyndale House; Author, *Zeal without Burnout* and *Trusting God in the Darkness*

"This is such an important and significant book for our current culture. With superb skill, Matt opens up the Scriptures in a way that engages with and challenges cultural norms. My heart was warmed, my spirit stirred and my mind stretched. It's so relevant for men and women of every stage. I just loved it!"

**PAUL DALE,** Senior Pastor, The Bridge Church, Sydney

"*Reclaiming Masculinity* is a radical book—radical because it's biblical. We live in a time when masculinity gets an eye roll and is diluted and blurred, but Matt Fuller gives readers an inviting, full-strength, 4K vision of what it means to be a man who follows the Son of Man."

**J.A. MEDDERS,** Director of Assessment for Acts 29; Author, *Humble Calvinism*

T0025988

"We desperately need wisdom to live out God's vision for masculinity. We need it in a way that steers clear of stereotypes yet seeks to take Scripture seriously. And we need to hear it from teachers who model that vision with humility, care and grace. Matt is such a man. This thought-provoking and practical volume will challenge and encourage you in equal measure."

**JASON ROACH,** Director of Ministries, London City Mission; Author, *Healing the Divides*

"I loved this book. It warmed my heart and encouraged my soul. The chapter on ambition had me praying with tears in my eyes."

**WILL STILEMAN,** Associate Rector, All Souls Langham Place, London

"Biblically rooted and practically illustrated, Matt Fuller's excellent book comes like a breath of fresh air into the current confusion surrounding modern manhood. Kind and gracious yet incisive and courageous, he not only honours Christian truth but also provides practical and accessible steps that we can follow. Here is a book that many have been waiting for and will be grateful to have."

**TERRY VIRGO,** Founder of Newfrontiers; Author, *God's Treasured Possession*

"Matt Fuller provides a much-needed voice of calm to the often-heated discussion of what it means to be masculine. Without sidestepping difficult issues, Matt pushes beyond simplistic and often negative caricatures of masculinity to present a positive biblical vision of what it means to thrive as a man created in God's image. Through judicious examination of the Scriptures and nuanced theological reflection, and driven by pastoral warmth, Matt provides hope and encouragement to all of us who are seeking to live as godly men in this age of confusion. I'm so pleased to have such an excellent resource to be able to commend to others."

**MALCOLM GILL,** Lead Pastor, Multicultural Bible Ministry, Sydney

"A brave and timely gem, packed with fresh and thought-provoking biblical insights and wholesome practical applications, and peppered with gripping stories and illustrations. Matt Fuller gives us a compelling vision of masculinity from God's word, for today's confused world."

**RICHARD COEKIN,** Senior Pastor, Dundonald Church, SW London; CEO, Co-Mission Church-Planting Network

# RECLAIMING
# MASCULINITY

## MATT FULLER

*For Andy and Jody:*

*Godly men, dear friends and epic godfathers*

*You have made an enormous difference to my life and to that of your godson*

Reclaiming Masculinity
© 2023 Matt Fuller

Published by:
The Good Book Company

thegoodbook.com | thegoodbook.co.uk
thegoodbook.com.au | thegoodbook.co.nz | thegoodbook.co.in

Unless indicated, all Scripture references are taken from the Holy Bible, New
International Version. Copyright © 2011 Biblica, Inc. Used by permission.

All rights reserved. Except as may be permitted by the Copyright Act, no part of this
publication may be reproduced in any form or by any means without prior
permission from the publisher.

Matt Fuller has asserted his right under the Copyright, Designs and Patents Act
1988 to be identified as author of this work.

ISBN: 9781784988647 | Printed in the UK

Cover design by André Parker

# CONTENTS

# INTRODUCTION:
# TO BE A MAN MEANS...
# WHAT, EXACTLY?

If you had to grab a pen now, how would you finish this sentence?

*"To be a man means..."*

No, really. Try to finish the sentence before you read any further. Don't feel awkward if you're uncertain what to say—most people struggle. It's actually pretty difficult, isn't it?

One journalist recently spent a few weeks asking 16-year-old boys in the UK that question. The responses varied:

*"You mean Yorkie bars and steel factories, that sort of thing?" Joel*

*"Doing what you believe to be right." Jesiah*

*"You stand up for yourself, but you also stand up for others." Sonny*

*"It's mainly about fitness and strength." Matt*

*"The stereotype's been put in our heads that we're supposed to be strong, not meant to allow any emotions, but I don't agree with that." Corrin*

*"The feeling of a lot of people my age is that to be a man, you have to be able to fight." Ty*

*"I think many boys my age are stuck, unsure." Clement*

*"I think a lot of mainstream politicians are afraid to really touch on masculinity, in case of maybe saying the wrong thing. And I can understand that. It's a very difficult thing to talk on. But I think there does need to be a place to be able to say that masculinity's a good thing. That masculinity can be admirable. Otherwise, we're just, sort of, just stranded." Joel* [1]

## SORT OF STRANDED

That's a shrewd comment from 16-year-old Joel! A lot of young men are indeed "sort of stranded". In a recent survey, only 2% of men aged 18-24 said they felt completely masculine.[2] Among those over 65 it was 56%. Yes, it's only a survey, in which "masculinity"

---

1 https://www.theguardian.com/lifeandstyle/2019/mar/09/a-lot-of-us-are-in-the-dark-what-teenage-boys-really-think-about-being-a-man (accessed November 28, 2022).

2 https://yougov.co.uk/topics/politics/articles-reports/2016/05/13/low-young-masculinity-britain. Other research suggests a similar generational gap exists in the US, although it is complicated by other divides there: https://www.theguardian.com/world/2016/may/31/masculinity-study-america-men-united-kingdom-yougov (both accessed November 28, 2022).

was not defined, and so it was a highly subjective self-evaluation. But clearly there are a lot of young men who, like Clement, are "stuck, unsure" about what it means to be a man.

That's quite a change in a few generations. Back in 1956, for instance, Professor Henry Higgins sang these words in *My Fair Lady* (and to be clear, the song was poking fun at the pompous Higgins and his inability to understand women):

*Why can't a woman be more like a man?*
*Men are so honest, so thoroughly square;*
*Eternally noble, historically fair;*
*Who, when you win, will always give your back a pat.*
*Why can't a woman be like that?*

My point is not (*at all*) that Higgins was right, or that things were better in the fifties. But in the fifties there was a clear idea of what it meant to be a man. In the 21st-century West, there simply isn't, and our culture is far more likely to ask, "Why can't a man be more like a woman?" "Traditional" male attributes such as competitiveness, stoicism (that is, bearing difficulties without complaint or displaying much emotion) and risk-taking are discouraged in classrooms and derided in sitcoms and films. The language of business management has shifted to emphasise "traditional" feminine virtues of empathy, co-operation and emotional intelligence. Women do better at school and a higher percentage go to university. Men are far more likely (to an alarming extent) to go to prison, become homeless or commit suicide.

Perhaps really we need to ask, "Why can't a man be more like a woman?"

Yet, in actual fact, probably more common is the claim that there is no difference between men and women at all. This becomes a rallying cry to ensure that we change the fact that men disproportionately hold places in boardrooms, in government and in industry. We're told that glass ceilings must be smashed and barriers broken down; women must "lean in" and men must make room. Anything men can do women can, should and must be doing too.

I keep hearing these two opinions, expressed in a variety of ways but basically boiling down to "Men and women are the same" and "Men should be more like women". The upshot is that we're getting a bit confused about what it means to be a man. No wonder only 2% of young men think they are completely masculine.

## IS MASCULINITY TOXIC?

In the last decade, the cultural mood music of the West has increasingly argued that masculinity is basically bad. A lot of people—men and women—have been hurt by or are angry about their own experience of masculinity. Enter "toxic masculinity" into the search box on Amazon and over 1,000 books will come up with that as a title or theme. In researching for this book, I've read a few of these books, and they often contain a sad story of an abusive or absent father and a distant or unemotional or violent form of masculinity. Often there's anger at the model of masculinity that has been presented to the author. It is clear that something *has* gone wrong, and a lot of men *have* abused their strength, leaving a lot of emotionally wounded wives and children, colleagues and friends. It's in that context that the American Psychological Association has also now declared that "traditional masculinity"—defined as stoicism, competitiveness, dominance and aggression—can be "psychologically harmful".[3]

I'm sure that a "traditional masculinity" can sometimes be harmful, and I am certainly not here to defend the abuses of the past. And I also want to argue that there's a difference between that definition of "traditional masculinity" and what we could call "biblical masculinity." But the type of masculinity the APA defines as traditional and harmful deserves defending for a moment. To say that some traits can be harmful if indulged excessively is not the same as saying that they always are. As I write this, we're approaching November 11th: Remembrance Day. In the UK, the majority of the population are wearing poppies to commemorate the sacrifice of those people who gave their lives to defend our country and its values. Chiefly, those people were men, and we honour and give thanks for their

3 https://www.apa.org/monitor/2019/01/ce-corner (accessed November 28, 2022).

stoicism and aggression during armed conflict. Clearly, then, these traits are not always bad. Competitiveness can be useful in driving innovation. If I'm in a building that's on fire, I'd like the firefighter to assert some dominance and order me around. So-called "masculine traits" can surely be good *or* bad, beneficial *or* abused, depending upon the context and how they are used.

## #SHAME

Nevertheless, there have without doubt been exposed in recent years some ugly expressions of masculinity that we should recoil from. There are indeed many men who should be ashamed of their behaviour. Perhaps we need to be slow to assume that we should not be included among them in some way and to some extent.

In the West, the #metoo movement has shone a spotlight on utterly unacceptable and disgraceful forms of sexual assault and harassment by dominant males. Many of the stories that have emerged have been appalling. In the UK, the *Everyone's Invited* website, which hit public consciousness in March 2021, presents a vast collection of stories about teenage girls being sexually assaulted and abused by teenage boys. It is genuinely shocking (an overused term, but appropriate here), with, at the time of writing, over 50,000 testimonies of abuse. It's an emotionally traumatic website to read. It led to accusations of "rape culture" in numerous schools, with some schools being mentioned in 170 testimonies of abuse.[4] It led to many parents wondering how on earth "their boys" could have behaved in such a way. Understandably, a vast amount was written about what men should not be like, and the cry went up, "We need to educate men how to behave". The problem was, I didn't read much by way of positive curriculum.

I did, however, read of one school assembly in Victoria, Australia, in which all male students were told to stand up and apologise for the behaviours of their sex that have hurt or offended girls and women.[5] Although the school principal later admitted that this was inappropriate, it reveals a cultural climate in which it can seem like a good idea to get a whole room of boys aged 11-18 to apologise, simply for being a male. They were essentially being told, "All men are culpable, all men are responsible, and all of you are potential offenders". No wonder so many men are stuck and unsure about what masculinity should look like. Are we meant to strive for masculinity at all?

I was struck by the humorous honesty of one middle-aged male journalist, who wrote:

*"What does it mean, then, to say we should educate men? ... With my daughters I know what the positive*

---

4 "Rape normal at private school, says dossier of 170 testimonies" https://www.thetimes.co.uk/article/c000d75a-8c16-11eb-a1a3-928d43a3bbc1?shareToken=38e0dd53617d7a6e4e614d27930da910 (accessed November 28, 2022).

5 https://news.sky.com/story/amp/schoolboys-made-to-apologise-for-stuff-we-didnt-do-during-assembly-about-sexual-assault-12260783 (accessed November 28, 2022).

*message is. 'You can do whatever boys can do and more.'
With boys though? I'd be lost. And I've been one for a
while now. You'd have thought I'd have figured it out."*[6]

How would you advise him? Should we be telling our sons,
and ourselves:

1. "Be more like girls"

2. "There is no difference between boys and girls"

Or can we find an ending to the sentence, *"To be a man
means..."*?

My argument is that it's not enough to say to young
men, "Stop acting like that". We need a positive vision of
masculinity. The lack of such a positive vision of being
male is now increasingly being recognised as a problem
in secular studies. A recent study by the UK-based group
Hope not Hate found that half of young men believe
that feminism "has gone too far and makes it harder
for men to succeed". Hope not Hate campaigns against
extremism. They commissioned the research because it
fears that aggressive anti-feminism is appealing to young
men feeling emasculated in an age of changing norms.
They need a positive vision of what it means to be a man.
Similarly, there is increased awareness that the horrific
misogyny (contempt for women) on "incel" (involuntary
celibate men) websites, and the popularity of misogynists

---

6 Hugo Rifkind, "How should men behave in age of #MeToo?" https://www.
  thetimes.co.uk/article/d7c71134-85ad-11eb-9186-403d3ffc3950?shareToke
  n=8f128df6b04f267466f60a547cd5791d (accessed November 28, 2022)

such as Andrew Tate (who owns and glories in the idea that his is a "toxic" masculinity) flows from the lack of a positive vision for masculinity.[7] Whatever you make of Jordan Peterson, the psychology professor, he is adored by many young men for telling them not much more than that being male means taking responsibility and living for a purpose. He is one of the few voices in mainstream culture giving young men a positive message.[8]

## LET'S GET POSITIVE

I want to reclaim the notion of masculinity from always being paired with the words "toxic" or "problematic". Equally, I want to do so without resorting to the negative aspects of the kind of masculinity which led to #metoo being necessary, which was expressed in a multitude of less extreme ways by so many of us, and which went virtually unchallenged for so long. I'm not here to argue for a return to the 1950s, as though that was some golden age for both men and women. What I want to briefly do in the next few chapters is outline a positive picture of biblical masculinity. What kind of man does *God* want you to be?

---

7 Libby Purves, "One lesson for schools is recruit male teachers" https://www.thetimes.co.uk/article/one-lesson-for-schools-is-recruit-male-teachers-9w9rj3cp2 (accessed November 28, 2022). Nick Staunton, "Andrew Tate: Selling masculinity to young men," https://brightonjournal.co.uk/andrew-tate-selling-masculinity-to-young-men/ (accessed January 11, 2022).

8 To clarify, I am not supporting everything he says. Jordan Peterson does not claim to be presenting a biblical view of manhood. He does, by God's common grace, get some things right and has clearly helped a lot of men.

The Bible teaches that there is more in common between the human sexes than there are differences. The Bible also teaches that men and women are different, and supports the idea that there are some traits which are more broadly male and some more broadly female and that there are some roles which are a better fit for men and some which are a better fit for women.

At this point, I want to frontload a few clarifications to help you read me kindly:

- I want to repeat that I am *not* arguing for a return to the past. I'm not simply hankering back to medieval times when men would ride to war on horses and sweep damsels off their feet. I don't think reclaiming masculinity is a zero-sum game in which men have to fight back against women. I would hope that female readers would be pleased about what they'll read in these chapters.

- A number of the differences between men and women are generalities. Men are *in general* taller than women. That does not mean that every man is taller than every woman. Men are *in general* stronger than women, but not every man is stronger than every woman. We will talk about male traits *in general* but shouldn't be thrown by the fact that some men don't demonstrate all of these traits, any more than we are thrown by meeting a man who is 5 feet tall or a woman who is 6 feet 6 inches. We can speak of generalities knowing that there are exceptions to every rule.

- I don't want to define men purely by taking biblical descriptions of husbands and wives and then using those to produce definitions of men and women. I think we can learn as much from looking at descriptions of "fathers", "brothers" and "friends". And these categories have something to say to all men, whether or not we're actually fathers or brothers. If a single man such as the apostle Paul can describe himself as a father to younger guys or whole churches, there must be something to learn about being a male from that.

- This is not a book about pornography. That is a huge topic on its own—and there will be many reading this whose next thing to read is a book that will help you in this area. I will only mention porn at a couple of points, but it is worth saying at the start that it is one hugely significant factor that is preventing Christian men living out a biblical masculinity.[9]

---

9 If you're someone who uses porn, or who is dealing with the effects of doing so in the past or wanting to help another guy who is struggling in this area, a good book to start with is Tim Chester, *Closing the Window: Steps to Living Porn-Free* (IVP, 2010). If you prefer audio, I know that people have found this talk by Winston Smith very helpful: https://www.ccef.org/shop/product/solo-sex-1/ (accessed January 26, 2023).

- I'm not here to beat you up. I've read enough books and listened to enough talks telling me that I'm not a "real man" and that I'm failing as a father and a husband. I know I am—I certainly don't get all of this right. You have my permission to throw the book across the room if you read any phrase that starts with "Real men..."

- I imagine this book will irritate everyone. Some will think that I'm far too specific on what it means to be male. Others will think me too vague. I'll be disagreeing with some of my close friends. But as long as we're not ignoring the clear teaching of Scripture, that's ok. As we'll see, quite a lot of heat comes from the fact that some of what it means to be masculine is culturally expressed and a matter of wisdom. I don't mind if you disagree with some of my conclusions as long as you've wrestled with the biblical model of wants it means to live as a godly man.

(Of course, in the end, if you *really* disagree with me, we could retreat into a sulky stoic silence or perhaps get competitive and have an aggressive fight. We could duke it out. That's what real men do. Oh. Sorry.)

That's the caveats out of the way. Let me return to where this chapter started. How would you finish the sentence "To be a man means..."?

More crucially, in fact, how would you finish the sentence...

*"To be a **godly** man means..."?*

My hope for you as you read this book is that you'll be able to complete that sentence. As you read this book, you'll find seven principles that describe a biblical, healthy, confident, helpful masculinity.

There will be complexities and nuances to wrestle with, as well as some more simple and straightforward things. You'll need, of course, to apply the principles to your own character, opportunities and circumstances. I'm really hoping that there will be many women reading this book, and I want to thank you for being here and to apologise in advance for the fact that whenever I say "you" from now on, I'm imagining a male reader.

So let's get on to Principle One: men really are different from women.

# PRINCIPLE #1
# MEN AND WOMEN REALLY ARE DIFFERENT
# [BUT DON'T EXAGGERATE]

**M**en and women have different brains.

That simple sentence could be the cue for some cheap gags or for outrage. But it is now viewed as an important fact in scientific research. To quote the *Journal of Neuroscience*, to ignore this fact would mean that "scientific discoveries that could benefit the health of both men and women would be hampered".[10] In other words, it is medically foolish to deny that men and women have different brains. To do so prevents each sex from receiving the care and advice that would benefit them most.

---

10 https://www.jneurosci.org/content/36/47/11817 (accessed November
   28, 2022). Since 2016 the US National Institutes of Health has refused
   to fund research which denies sex as a biological variable. In other words,
   all research must show results for men and women separately in order
   to aid clinical assessments. While this is the majority view in this area of
   research, there remain dissenting voices. See, for example, Gina Rippon,
   *The Gendered Brain*, (Bodley Head, 2019).

It's not just neuroscientists who believe this. Psychologists have uncovered dozens of ways in which men and women differ in their thinking, emotions and behaviour (ways that are not better or worse—just different!). For years, the prevailing argument went that this was produced by sexist cultures and assumptions about men and women that were projected onto children. That is now generally rejected. Secular research suggests that sex differences in most psychological traits are larger in cultures with a more egalitarian sex-role culture.[11] To take one example, more egalitarian cultures, like Norway and Sweden, produce comparatively fewer women pursuing careers in science, technology, engineering and maths (STEM subjects).[12] Empirical evidence indicates that when there is complete freedom to choose, without economic or social pressures, men and women tend to lean in different directions.

You can chase down some of the research yourself, but the headline is this: men and women *in general* are wired differently (those two words in italics may become tedious, but I'm going to keep inserting them). There is plenty of research which suggests that this is not down to cultural views of gender roles. There is a male way of being human that is woven into every part of a man's DNA. Men and women are different—yet, culturally, we're scared to say it because of the nagging fear that

---

11 https://link.springer.com/chapter/10.1007/978-3-319-09384-0_11 (accessed November 28, 2022).

12 https://journals.sagepub.com/doi/abs/10.1177/0956797617741719?journ alCode=pssa (accessed November 28, 2022).

when we say "different", people hear "not equal", and so begins the descent towards abuse: "You're a bigot... You should be cancelled..." and so on.

## REACTING AND OVERREACTING

If the wider culture is uncertain about how to express masculinity, so is the church. In the last couple of decades, some have reacted against what they perceived as an effeminate church culture by stressing that Jesus was an alpha male with callused hands and big biceps who loved to turn tables over and confront opponents. The intention here was good. There was a concern that men would be turned off by a feeble church culture, and so church needed to become "guy friendly". However, this emphasis on a "Fighting Jesus" seemed too frequently to go hand in hand with a domineering and bullying style of church leadership. More generally, there was a danger of presenting a one-dimensional view of masculinity which left many guys thinking, "But I'm nothing like that. I like baking, ballet and book clubs."

In the UK there has recently been a condemnation of "Muscular Christianity", which, critics say, grew out of the Victorian boarding-school training-for-empire mindset. While this approach is perhaps not as crude as "Fighting Jesus", the allegation is that it produces a view of real manliness as requiring a stiff-upper-lip mentality which does not admit weakness or ask for help. Some leaders have tended towards a culture of "We're in a fight against liberal Christianity. Support me or you'll be denounced as 'not one of us'." While there is truth in this accusation, I'm still personally unsure about how widespread the problem is.

But now, as a consequence of these exaggerated forms of Christian masculinity, it seems to me that the pendulum is swinging hard in the other direction, and many churches are nervous about articulating any differences between men and women at all. Because we are nervous of exaggerating the differences between the sexes (a historical problem), it has become easier to say nothing at all about them being different (a modern problem). To put it another way, at some points in history the devil attacks the equality of men and women, while at other points he attacks the difference between them.

We need to avoid either exaggerating the difference between the sexes or minimising it. This is quite hard to do. In an effort to keep things fairly simple while trying to avoid becoming simplistic, we can outline three different approaches Christians tend to take:

1. There are no significant differences between men and women; we should simply aspire to be mature Christians. The fruit of the Spirit is not seen in male traits or female traits—love, joy, peace, patience, self-control and so on are not gender-specific. We should be concerned with these things, not with what it means to be a *male* or *female* Christian. We could call this the "no difference" approach.

2. Only two New Testament passages are explicit about different roles for men and women—Ephesians 5:22-33 and 1 Timothy 2:11-15—and even then, these texts don't have in view all men and all women, but just marriage and church leadership.[13] There is not a lot to say about men and women in general, and the Bible doesn't say anything to guys if they're not married or a church elder (except in terms of preparing them to one day, perhaps, be one or both). Let's call this the "only two differences" position.

3. There are inherent differences between men and women that manifest themselves throughout life. There is a pattern of being a man that should be pursued in all areas. Men should always lead, and all women should submit. This should be obvious in all areas of a marriage: for example, the husband should always drive the family car and be the chief breadwinner. Let's call this the "differences are clear and must be maintained in a wide-ranging fashion" approach.

I am generalising here for the sake of simplicity, but most Christians are, more or less, in one of these groups. Yet there are problems with all of them. Let's turn to one of

---

13 Many would also point to 1 Corinthians 14:34-35 and 14:34-35 as teaching that men and women have different roles in church, and 1 Peter 3:1-7 and Colossians 3:18-19, which echo the teaching of Ephesians 5. But this doesn't affect the simple structure I'm describing here—marriage and church leadership are the only settings within which there is difference.

the more neglected passages, in terms of gender roles, to see a few of them.

*Just as a nursing mother cares for her children, so we cared for you. Because we loved you so much, we were delighted to share with you not only the gospel of God but our lives as well. Surely you remember, brothers and sisters, our toil and hardship; we worked night and day in order not to be a burden to anyone while we preached the gospel of God to you. You are witnesses, and so is God, of how holy, righteous and blameless we were among you who believed. For you know that we dealt with each of you as a father deals with his own children, encouraging, comforting and urging you to live lives worthy of God, who calls you into his kingdom and glory. (1 Thessalonians 2:7-12)*

Three things are worth noting:

- Paul is quite content to describe himself acting as a mother and as a father. He displays classically feminine traits—nursing and caring—as well as traditionally masculine ones—exhorting and urging. He undermines the idea in Position Three above, of differences between men and women being *really* clear, stark and binary. Healthy men, he is saying, will display some "feminine" traits.

- Yet at the same time, Paul is content to associate "nursing" language with mothers and "exhorting" language with fathers, along the lines of traditional gender roles. He seems to think that this is natural, and so he rejects the concept of "no difference" between male and female (Position One). He recognises that some traits are more naturally associated with mothers and some more naturally with fathers, even while saying that he displayed both of them in his care for the Christians in Thessalonica.

- Paul, as a single man, adopts the language of being a father to others. This raises a problem with Position 2, which seems to make it impossible to demonstrate a biblical masculinity unless you are married or in church leadership. It seems to rule out any concept of *inherent* maleness (beyond biology). That position limits distinctive masculinity to certain roles and offers little to a single man about what it means to act in a masculine way (or, indeed, to a married man outside of his marriage or an elder outside of church).

I lived with Position 2 ("only two differences") for a long time. I would have described myself as complementarian (as I still do), holding to the belief that God made men and women equal in value and dignity and also different in certain responsibilities and roles, so as to need one another. But I struggled to articulate what that meant outside of marriage or church leadership. Even in those two areas, the differences felt a little bit arbitrary. I was content to trust that God knew best how things should run in the world he'd made, but I felt a little embarrassed, especially by the differences in church leadership roles of 1 Timothy 2. Although I never vocalised it or had it clear in my head, I think the position I held was a little like this:

"God says that men and women should have different roles. I know—weird, right? I certainly do not mean different roles in the way that an older generation behaved—that just looked sexist and unhealthy. But God does say men and women have different roles. So let's trust him and operate this way, even though we feel a bit awkward about it."

The problem is that embarrassment is unlikely to coexist with a sustainable living out of the Bible. So I went back to consider how those commands for marriage and church flow out of what is inherent to being male and female—how they are natural and fitting rather than being arbitrary or unfair; how God desires us to flourish as *male* believers and *female* believers, and not only as believers. So, I want to persuade you of Position 2.5. We could call it "Differences are real and unchanging, but show themselves culturally and therefore differently." Ignoring these differences dishonours God (see 1 Corinthians 11:3-4) and prevents us from thriving as men and women. Yet being rigid in their application can be harmful and just as easily prevent our flourishing.

## IN GENERAL, WE'RE DIFFERENT

1 Thessalonians 2 is not alone in assuming these differences exist without spelling them out. There are numerous New Testament passages which assume that certain ways of relating are more obviously male, while others are more naturally female. Look at the language attached to fathers.

> Even if you had ten thousand guardians in Christ, you do not have many fathers, for in Christ Jesus I became your father through the gospel. (1 Corinthians 4:15)

> But you know that Timothy has proved himself, because as a son with his father he has served with me in the work of the gospel. (Philippians 2:22)

> I appeal to you for my son Onesimus, whose father I became while I was in chains. (Philemon v 10)[14]

There is an assumption in all these verses that some patterns of behaviour are connected to fathers. Paul adopts the title of "father" with regard to both the church at Corinth and younger men such as Timothy and Onesimus. He does not choose teacher, guardian, mother, friend, counsellor. It is striking that a single man so readily reaches for the language of father to express his teaching, leading and mentoring. It implies that within any man there is the potential for acting in a specifically *father-like* role and that any man can express this sensibly when single.

---

14 This is a more natural rendering of the verb *gennao* than the NIV's "who became my son while I was in chains".

There are further implied differences in 1 Timothy 5 (which we'll return to applying when we reach Principle 6):

*Do not rebuke an older man harshly, but exhort him as if he were your father. Treat younger men as brothers, older women as mothers, and younger women as sisters, with absolute purity. (1 Timothy 5:1-2)*

Is there anything distinctive about being a son rather than a daughter? A brother rather than a sister? A man rather than a woman? Paul thinks that there is.

In a similar vein, the writer to the Hebrews assumes that a father will be the parent primarily concerned with discipline.

*Endure hardship as discipline; God is treating you as his children. For what children are not disciplined by their father? (Hebrews 12:7)*

Finally, there is also something implied beyond the constraints of marriage in 1 Peter 3:

*Husbands, in the same way be considerate as you live with your wives, and treat them with respect as the weaker partner and as heirs with you of the gracious gift of life, so that nothing will hinder your prayers. (1 Peter 3:7)*

The way that husbands are to treat their wives "with respect" is rooted in two things: first, that wives are co-heirs with their husbands. There is no sense of inferiority as they are of equal value. Second, that wives are weaker (which I take to mean physically weaker. She may be smarter, godlier and funnier than her husband!). There is something in the different physical characteristics of men and women that should affect how they relate to one another.

This must surely have some application outside of marriage, since it speaks to a general difference between the sexes. To state the obvious, a man does not become physically stronger when he marries. There must, therefore, be something in the physical strength of men which they need to consider when they relate to women. They must be conscious of not abusing their strength, but rather use it to "be considerate" (literally "act according to knowledge"). This warning reveals that there is something inherent about the strength of a man that can be used virtuously or used abusively. (We'll see when we get to Principles Five and Six that this strength is meant to be harnessed to protect.)

Overall, there is a presumption in the New Testament that *in general* there are certain patterns of behaviour that are more closely associated with fathers, brothers and men alongside other patterns more closely aligned with mothers, sisters and women. This is rarely explained; it is simply assumed. It makes it hard to read the New Testament and say that men and women are interchangeable.

None of these things make men better or worse than women—just different. And the Lord wants us to accept and enjoy the difference.

## OPENING CAR DOORS AND WEARING HATS

I think we know instinctively that men and women are different—but we don't know how to say that without tipping over into being overly prescriptive and saying that all men must be a certain way. Working out what this looks like is far more difficult, and that is because the difference between *timeless truths* and *cultural manifestations of those timeless truths* is often highly significant.

This can explain why different generations are often bewildered by one another. For example, I was surprised to be asked a little while ago, by someone in their twenties, whether a man should open a car door for a woman. I think that most people under the age of 50 find that a weird question even to ask. But 50 years ago, most people would have said yes: it was the gentlemanly thing to do. 150 years ago no one was asking the question as there were no cars. There can be no biblically "correct" answer to the question of a man opening a door for a woman. The cultural context will determine what is appropriate. Often what is viewed as a demonstration of masculinity may simply be a passing fad.

And to some extent, for holding the door in the 20th- and 21st-century West, we could substitute hair styles and head coverings in 1st-century Corinth. 1 Corinthians 11 will prevent us from defining masculinity by our culture, upbringing and role models. It's a passage that shows that the differences between men and women are timeless and real, but that culturally they are manifested differently:

*I praise you for remembering me in everything and for holding to the traditions just as I passed them on to you. But I want you to realise that the head of every man is Christ, and the head of the woman [wife] is man [husband], and the head of Christ is God. Every man who prays or prophesies with his head covered dishonours his head. (1 Corinthians 11:2-4)*[15]

Your instinct here may be "No one cares about hat (or hair) etiquette in the modern West". That is usually true—and it's a key element in interpreting this passage rightly. Paul is discussing a cultural application of a biblical truth. What was on your head mattered in Corinth in the 1st century. It does not in the 21st-century West. Yet the attitude in your heart most certainly does.

It seems as if some people in Corinth were saying it was outdated for wives in church to cover their heads when they were equal with their husbands. Why should men and women be distinguished by what they wear? Meanwhile, others were finding the lack of head coverings offensive.

In steps Paul...

Question: *Paul, why do we distinguish between men and women when you've told us that we're equal in Christ?*

---

15 "Head" could potentially mean source as in "the head of a river", and that might be true, as verse 8 expresses "woman came from man". However, we cannot say that God the Father is the source of Christ, as that would deny the eternal nature of the Son of God. In this context then, "head" is far more likely to mean "authority", as in the truth that Jesus has authority over the church.

Answer: *You'll dishonour God and your spouse if you ignore gender differences.*

If men fail to live appropriately as men, we will dishonour the Lord (v 4). We really do need to get this right, in a manner suitable for the 21st century and not the 16th. (I imagine Henry VIII thought he was very manly, but seriously, those breeches and codpieces are not going to cut it these days.)

## HONOURING IN YOUR CULTURE

It's fairly clear that verse 3 sets up three relationships in parallel:

- The head of every man is Christ.
- The head of the wife is the husband.[16]
- The head of Christ is God.

These relationships are not all the same! Christ created all humans, not just men. Men, or husbands, did not create women, or wives. God the Father did not create God the Son. That is not the comparison Paul is making; rather it is that each "head" should be honoured.

---

16 Most translations will include the two alternatives husband/man and wife/woman as a footnote. It is only the context which can tell us how to translate the two Greek words *andros* and *gynaikos*. Personally, I'm persuaded that it makes more sense to translate this as "the head of the wife is the husband", chiefly because Paul has the same thought in Ephesians 5:23: "The husband is the head of the wife as Christ is the head of the church".

That's the timeless truth. And this honouring is going to be displayed in culturally accepted ways:

*Every man who prays or prophesies with his head covered dishonours his head. But every woman [or wife] who prays or prophesies with her head uncovered dishonours her head—it is the same as having her head shaved. For if a woman [wife] does not cover her head, she might as well have her hair cut off; but if it is a disgrace for a woman [wife] to have her hair cut off or her head shaved, then she should cover her head. (1 Corinthians 11:4-6)*

How do we know that what's on your head is a cultural application? Because elsewhere in the Bible God has no problem with men having their heads covered. Notably, in Old Testament Israel the high priest was commanded to cover his head (Exodus 39:31). Nazirites had long hair as a sign of dedication to God (Numbers 6:5). So it cannot be that the prohibition here on men having heads uncovered or having long hair is a timeless principle. It must be something cultural—and archaeological evidence suggests that for a married Corinthian woman to have had her head uncovered was an indication that she was leaving the marriage or was sexually available to other men.[17] In 1st-century Corinth (unlike in Old Testament Israel or in

---

17 Views will vary among Christians on how much weight to give to extra-biblical evidence. My own view is, certainly not the same weight as the Bible—but if God has, in his sovereignty, given us help in understanding, we should make some use of it. There is some evidence that in the 1st-century Mediterranean, only pagan priests would cover their heads in worship and grow long hair. This is not determinative, but it is interesting.

the 21st-century West), whether you wore a hat made a statement that everyone who lived in that culture would understand, about whether you honoured your spouse (and, in doing so, the Lord). This was especially obvious when a woman was praying or prophesying, as that was when people would be looking at her.

## DIFFERENT AND INTERDEPENDENT

*⁷ [For] A man ought not to cover his head, since he is the image and glory of God; but woman is the glory of man. ⁸ For man did not come from woman, but woman from man; ⁹ neither was man created for woman, but woman for man. ¹⁰ It is for this reason that a woman [wife] ought to have authority over her own head, because of the angels.*

*¹¹ Nevertheless, in the Lord woman [wife] is not independent of [husband] man, nor is [husband] man independent of woman [wife]. ¹² For as woman came from man, so also man is born of woman.*

*(1 Corinthians 11:7-12)*

The cultural application of covering hair is grounded in the creation account. In the original Greek, both verses 7 and 8 begin with "for" or "because" (see ESV). There was a difference in the creation of men and women, and this difference is to be recognised, acknowledged and celebrated. Again, there is a subtlety to the argument:

- Man is the image and glory of God.

- Woman is the glory of man (not the image).

Woman is the glory of man because she was taken from him and made for him. Adam was the firstborn, with all the responsibilities which that involved, and Eve was made so that he could carry out those responsibilities. He couldn't do that on his own.

We might expect verse 10 to say, *Therefore, wives, cover your heads.* In fact, Paul says the wife should have authority over her head—meaning she should "take responsibility" or "do the right thing"—because the angels are, in some sense, watching what takes place when the church has gathered. This is not a passage about taking decisions in the home or who does which job around the house. It is about wives acknowledging and honouring their husbands when the church gathers. In Corinth this was manifested in wives covering their hair.

Verses 11-12 then immediately prevent an exaggerated interpretation of what Paul is saying. Husbands and wives—and, indeed, men and women more generally—are *interdependent*. We need one another. Paul does not simply shut women down from praying or prophesying. He wants to fully integrate women and their gifts into the experience of church meetings; and he wants this done in a way which, if they are married, does not undermine their husbands.

Verses 13-15 return to the stress on difference. Paul asks, "Does not the very nature of things teach you that if a man has long hair, it is a disgrace to him?" (v 14)—which suggests that something deep down within us knows that men and women are different and that this should be displayed in physical appearance.

## SO WHAT?

All of which should lead us to ask, "Ok, but practically, what are the implications of all this for us today?"

First, there is a general application to men and women in general. It is appropriate for men to dress in a male way and women to dress in a female way. But this can vary in different cultures. Back in the ancient world, Greeks in their dress-like togas mocked the Persian armies for wearing trousers; trousers were effeminate and only ridiculous men wore them. (I can't help but think the Greeks would have felt differently if they had had freezing winters with howling winds blowing around their exposed parts.)

Manifesting a biblical view of manhood in London looks different in 2022 from how it did in 1922. It will also look different depending on where you are in the world. Cultural expressions of manhood are different in London compared to Rwanda or China—so to be faithful to the Bible, the practical outworking of what Christian men wear and how we honour our wives *must* look different in the modern West compared to, say, Central Asia. (And, of course, even within one city at one time, there are different cultures, not just one.)

Second, there is an application to wives: to avoid signals which within the culture suggest a lack of respect; and an application to husbands: to be wary of undermining our wives. How this should look is very difficult to define because culture is always shifting. For example, I remember years ago my wife and I giving a lift to an older and much respected pastor. He was genuinely shocked that my wife drove—to him this was a cultural symbol of male leadership. For my generation, it was neither here nor there.

Or to take a more common example, some Christians are strongly of the view that wives should not go out to do salaried work but be home-focused. That may be great in some cultures, but I don't think the Bible requires that, and I'm not sure how that model applies to the majority of families in a city like London, where, given housing costs, it is increasingly rare that a family can live off of one salary (or indeed in many cultures across the world where mothers still have to work in the fields).[18] Or, to take another example, sometimes older generations might suggest that men don't show weakness—they plough on. Yet a younger generation might value authenticity far more, and being honest about our shortcomings can be profoundly helpful in a church!

Understanding that there is a difference between *timeless truths* and *cultural manifestations* of those truths will cause us to be a little more kind in listening to other cultures

---

18 I'm surprised how much heat this issue can generate! Certainly in London there often seems to be a lot of defensiveness for families about their choices here—whether the wife works in paid employment or not. I think it's good to assume that everyone's financial and family circumstances are different and that it's unwise to project your situation onto another family without taking time to understand them.

and generations. I don't intend to go to Rwanda and tell the Christians there that the ways in which they manifest masculinity are outdated simply because they're not how I express mine in the UK. If you're in your twenties, don't rudely tell the 60-year-old that his views of what it means to be a man are "obviously wrong"; if you're in your sixties, don't assume that your generation is better at being men. You may find that you and those you criticise agree on what the Bible teaches, but each side simply differs in how their generation applies it.

Still, timeless truths remain true for all time. In our cultural moment in the West, it is important to resist the fashionable opinion that gender is non-binary. No— there are men and women, and we should delight in the differences.[19] Christians will want to resist trends towards androgyny in dress or make-up. It should be obvious, from how we look, that Christian men are male. We will want to celebrate the differences between men and women and model them in attitude and dress; and in church, we will want to honour our spouses in what we do, how we dress, and how we speak.

"Being a godly man means…" We've established that it's ok to actually begin a sentence that way. There are differences between men and women. Now we can start to fill in the rest of the sentence.

---

19 A helpful introduction to that topic is Vaughan Roberts, *Transgender* (The Good Book Company, 2017).

# PRINCIPLE #2
# TAKE RESPONSIBILITY

**A** while ago a middle-aged guy at church made the following observation:

*"For much of my week I'm a leader in the office. People look to me to set the direction and ultimately take responsibility. Yet when I'm at home, I collapse. I'm exhausted, and so I passively allow the family to drift wherever they want. I've started to wonder if I'm modelling to my kids that work is where the action is and I serve the people there, and then at home I have no energy to lead and I don't want to be responsible. I wonder if they'll learn from me that fathers earn money but mothers lead the family. I wonder what impact that might have."*

There's a guy who recognises that he ought to be leading at home in some way.

Another friend recently lamented to me, "My adult sons seem to drift along with no great life plan. I wish they'd marry or buy a house... or buy a dog or even a hamster. Anything, really, that made them take some responsibility."

The desires of a 50-year-old for his sons are not automatically more godly than the life choices of a 20-something-year-old (particularly when it comes to owning a hamster). But there *is* something inherently and biblically masculine about taking responsibility.

## DIFFERENTLY HE CREATED THEM

As we start to flesh out a biblical conclusion to the sentence "To be a godly man means…" I want to highlight some of the differences described in the creation of man and woman in Genesis 1 – 3. Then we'll spend the rest of this chapter and the next three in drawing out three themes in particular.

That there *are* differences in the way God created the first man and the first woman is obvious. What those differences mean is slightly less so. What follows are some observations—I'm not yet drawing any conclusions:

1. The man and the woman are created from different material. The man is created from "the dust of the ground", and "the LORD God … breathed into his nostrils the breath of life" (Genesis 2:7). By contrast, the woman is made from the man (v 21-22). As we've seen, this difference is held up as being important in 1 Corinthians 11:8.

2. They are created at different times; the man came first. This is held to be significant in how churches function in 1 Timothy 2:11-13.

3. The man is given responsibility for the garden before the creation of the woman (Genesis 2:15) and consequently is held accountable for the first sin of humanity (3:17; see Romans 5:12-14).

4. The man is given responsibility before the creation of the woman for keeping the law (Genesis 2:16-17). He is forbidden to eat from the tree of the knowledge of good and evil. When this law is broken, God addresses and condemns Adam, not the couple jointly (Genesis 3:17).

5. There is a one-sided emphasis upon the man leaving his father and mother and being united to his wife (2:24). She is not said to leave her father and mother in the same way.

6. They are created in different places. He is made outside of the garden, while she is made within the garden (v 8, 22).

7. They each have a slightly different focus to their work. He is to work in the garden and protect it (v 15), while she is the necessary helper in his task. One aspect of this is in childbearing. No other creature could help the man with this. This slightly different leaning to their work becomes more obvious when we see the specific ways in which, having sinned, they are cursed. The man is cursed in his labour of working and cultivating the ground. The woman is cursed in her task of childbearing. (Don't run ahead with your own conclusions here; I'm still simply

making observations.) This is held to be significant in 1 Timothy 2:15.

8. The man is cursed for a specific reason, while the woman is not. He is told that he is cursed "because you [singular] listened to your wife and ate fruit from the tree about which I commanded you [singular]" (Genesis 3:17). Rather than lead the woman in obedience to a command she had not been given, he had followed her into sin.

These are clear and real differences. Importantly for the theme of this chapter, the man is given responsibility to lead in a way in which the woman is not. That responsibility is most obviously a *spiritual* responsibility to lead. The man's responsibility to keep God's commandment and his culpability for the failure of both of them is the most obvious feature of the leadership he is given.

Genesis 1 prevents us from exaggerating the extent of this. Before these distinctions between the man and the woman are introduced in Genesis 2, we have already been told in Genesis 1:27 that both men and women are created in the image of God—jointly. Verse 28 immediately stresses what the man and woman receive *together*: "God blessed *them* and said to *them*, 'Be fruitful and increase in number; fill the earth and subdue it'" (emphasis added).

So, when we read the whole of Genesis 1 – 3 together, we're led to say that...

1. the first man and the first woman are jointly given the task of superintending the earth

and that...

2. the man bears responsibility for this task in a way that the woman does not. In particular, he is responsible for giving a spiritual lead in trusting and obeying the word of God.

So... what does this practically mean?

- It *must* have some application to marriage (as this is a pattern for marriage before the fall).

- It *may* have some echo of application to single men. (I think it does, and we'll return to this at the end of the chapter.)

- It *definitely* has an application to church life (which we'll consider when we reach Principle 4).

## RESPONSIBILITY IN MARRIAGE

The New Testament takes what is described in the first three chapters of the Bible and makes it explicit that a husband has responsibility for leading in marriage:

*Wives, submit yourselves to your own husbands as you do to the Lord. **For the husband is the head of the wife** as Christ is the head of the church.*

*(Ephesians 5:22-23, emphasis added)*

At this point we'd best pause, because we may have a bit of a problem with how we hear the word "head" or "leadership".[20] Sometimes these verses have been taken as an excuse for a husband to be overbearing and controlling in his marriage, rather than a command to take a lead that is kind and for the benefit of his wife. The problem comes if we separate the responsibility that a husband has (being the head) from the model that the Bible provides for leaders: "Husbands, love your wives, just as Christ loved the church and gave himself up for her" (v 25).

We need to be clear that while the Bible grounds the fact of a husband's headship in creation, this leadership is *defined* by Christ's sacrificial love. To paraphrase C.S. Lewis, if a husband wears a crown, it is a crown of thorns.[21] Jesus leads by sacrificing. He leads at a cost to himself. He leads by bearing a burden that his bride could not. By way of imperfect analogy, while many of us will have known bosses at work who have failed to lead or who led in an overbearing way, hopefully lots of us will have experienced a boss who takes on the burden of leading, for which we're grateful. It certainly is possible to lead a marriage in a way which is a blessing to a wife, which removes burdens from them, builds them up and liberates them to serve in multiple ways. (Note: Don't, on the basis

20 I'm using the language of "leadership" rather than "headship" as it's a more readily understandable word. You can read the technical commentaries about what precisely "headship" means. But in simple language, it means leadership.

21 C.S. Lewis, *The Four Loves* (William Collins, 2015), p 100.

of this chapter, declare you're the boss of your home—it's just an analogy!)

Love does not abdicate; love does not dominate. No husband gets this right all the time. Most of us will lean in one direction or other—we'll tend towards being overbearing and dominating, or we'll tend towards laziness and abdication. Neither is better than the other. There is a subculture in some of the Christian circles I've been in which suggests that while being overbearing isn't ideal, it's better to fall off the horse on that side than to be lazy. But surely it depends on how badly you're falling. I've had a guy tell me proudly how he went through his wife's diary on a regular basis, telling her what she could and couldn't do. I don't think that's sacrificial leadership; I think that's creepy. I've had to get involved in a situation in which a husband refused to let his wife have a bank card and only gave her limited amounts of cash to spend each week. That's not sacrificial leadership; that's emotional, as well as financial, abuse. The love of Christ is sacrifice. It is grace. It is patience, not angry frustration. It is kindness, not manipulation. It's gentle and kind, not forceful or demanding. It's life-giving, not life-restricting.

At times, in some cultures, abusive husbands have been tolerated in a way that we find abhorrent today and that the Bible has always said is unacceptable. At times, this has been true of Christian husbands. We need to be honest and say that this is still true in many homes today—including in Christian homes, including in evangelical Christian homes (more than most of us are aware). If you are, deep down, wondering if your own conduct as a husband may fall this side of the Christlike line, please stop, pray, and speak to someone who knows and loves you well enough to tell you if and where you need to repent and change. If you are a woman reading this and recognise some symptoms of controlling or abusive behaviour, I pray you'll feel able to speak up.

There is an opposite error, too, which is for Christian husbands to drift towards abdicating our responsibility to lead. C.S. Lewis again helpfully observes that men think of unselfishness as not giving trouble to others, whereas women think of it chiefly as taking trouble off of others.[22] If there is some truth to that observation (and I think there is), then the female perspective is far closer to the biblical view of love.

Paul seems to be hinting at male laziness in Ephesians 5:

> *He who loves his wife loves himself. After all, no one ever hated their own body, but they feed and care for their body, just as Christ does the church. (v 28-29)*

When I get hungry (or, occasionally, "hangry"), then there is no way I'm going to neglect my wellbeing, and I don't need anyone to tell me not to neglect it. Yet sometimes I need reminding to not neglect my wife. Twenty years ago, when I was a few years into marriage, a friend of mine

---

22 C.S. Lewis, *The Screwtape Letters* (Collins, 2012), chapter 26.

began a conversation like this: "Matt, do you mind if I make an observation on your marriage?"

You know it's not going to be good when someone begins a conversation like that! Adopting a neutral voice, I replied, "Not at all, Tim, go for it". So he did...

*"It seems to me that your marriage works like this: 'I'll work, work, work, and then play, play, play, and every so often I'll look up and check: Wife ok? Yep, I think so. Great—back to work, work, work; then play, play, play.'*

*"Or you'll say, 'Wife ok? Oh dear, no. Let's do a little bit of reactive care, until she's ok. And then I can get back to work, work, work; then play, play, play.'*

*"Matt, I wonder if that's a biblical view of sacrificially loving your wife. It looks a little bit like doing whatever you want and only troubling to do some repair work when it's necessary."*

That stung. But he was right. It was one of the most helpful rebukes I've ever had. Husbands are meant to help their wives flourish spiritually and generally by sacrificing for their good. Part of that is kindly addressing the things that are troubling your wife: she wants a shelf put up— why not do it (or for some of us, find someone who can)? Part of that sacrifice is taking a lead.

This all flows out of how we are made—Paul reveals that Genesis 2 has been in the background all along:

*For this reason a man will leave his father and mother and*
*be united to his wife, and the two will become one flesh.*
*(Ephesians 5:31)*

I think that the logic in the flow of Ephesians 5 is that husbands and wives are one flesh, and so they should function as one flesh, not as two autonomous individuals running parallel lives. To function as one flesh requires one head. That head is the husband, and so he needs to lead the marriage in such a way that they are one flesh, not two individuals. It is in this sense that the call for wives to "submit" is to be primarily understood.

Years ago, before we had children, we hit the buffers a little. Finances were tight when I was in a junior role at church, and my wife was working five long days a week. With church commitments added on top, the wheels came off. On this occasion I actually took the initiative to find a way forward. (I confess that really isn't always the case.) We talked about the options for making each week a little more sustainable and decided together that it would really help if, in our particular circumstances and given our particular financial situation, she dropped down to four days a week. It was no good leading parallel lives— we needed to operate more as one flesh.

## WHAT GENTLE LEADING LOOKS LIKE

In some Christian circles, the responsibility for a husband to take a lead seems to be interpreted through a middle-class 19th-century lens, so that the only acceptable model is for the husband to go out to work while the wife stays at home and churns butter while home-schooling their ten children. Now, there is nothing wrong with doing that. But there's something wrong with saying that that's the only way to be a godly husband.

So what *should* it look like?

The big picture is easy: Ephesians 5 is clear that we should lead like Jesus! He loves his church and gave himself up for her. He has made his people holy and is resolutely and unstoppably committed to presenting them without stain, wrinkle or any other blemish. He is at work to feed, nourish and sustain.

The detail is a little harder. For many years, my wife and I led the premarital preparation evenings for engaged couples. Upon reflection, I think we were far too detailed in what we said roles within marriage should look like, in particular with regard to the instruction that wives should submit and husbands love. I now think that husbands sacrificially leading and wives gently submitting can be done in many different healthy ways.

If you're married, your wife is to submit to your kind leading. This is not a matter of competency or temperament. The reason is theological. Paul is envisaging a glimpse of Eden before the fall. It is less a matter of the husband taking authority over the wife and more a picture of the wife following her husband's lead in serving the kingdom of God.

I don't think it's helpful to define the husband's leadership or responsibility prescriptively. But if you are a husband, your spiritual leadership must have *some definition* within *your* marriage. For the health of the relationship, the two of you should be able to express something of what it means for you to provide a sacrificial lead. So, if you're a husband, here's the question:

*How do you provide a gentle spiritual leadership to your wife?*

If you can't find anything to say, then maybe that's because you're failing to lead and are asking your wife to bear more burden in the marriage than she should.

If you did answer, why not ask your wife if she agrees, and if it is a helpful way of serving her? That must be a part of what Peter means by living "with your wife according to knowledge" (1 Peter 3:7, my translation). I think it is unlikely that husbands will get their leadership right without asking for some kind and gentle feedback! So, ask your wife for her view on what it would look like for you to lead lovingly and well.

My own wife happens to work part-time in the financial City of London, and I don't think anyone would describe her as passive. She's a whirlwind of activity. When I ask her how she wants me to take responsibility in our marriage, she will commonly say, "I want you to take time to understand me. I want you to know my anxieties and concerns. I want you to be available for me—

which sometimes means making yourself unavailable for others." I honestly can't think of many important decisions that we haven't chatted through and reached a conclusion together through that process. I think that my role is to ensure those conversations happen, rather than allowing the marriage to drift aimlessly.

I think that's true for a lot of marriages. There's often something that needs addressing—differing views on the future, a problem with the kids, or a very common drifting apart with no great reason for it happening. Husbands, we need to ensure that the issue is addressed, that we understand our wives, and that we sacrifice for them.

Let me give some practical (and real) examples of providing a necessary lead. These are not everyday events but those rare moments when a marriage reaches an impasse.

After a number of years of failing to conceive, a husband and wife begin to consider IVF treatment. They each come to different conclusions on the ethics of carrying out IVF. The husband believes it's ok, but the wife doesn't think the treatment of embryos in IVF makes it feasible to be done in good conscience. So, what should they do? A failure to agree means that by default they will follow the wife's position. That is not leading. I think that the husband needs to ensure that they have taken time to read and pray about the issue together and to understand one another's position carefully. It may well be that he needs to bring a third party into the conversation to help them navigate it. If, after a period of time, they both still hold to their positions, then I imagine he would have to sacrifice his desire to pursue IVF.

Another couple have very different views on how to parent their kids. The wife has grown up in a Christian family where she called her parents by their first names and there was relatively little discipline. She valued the chance to grow up making (and learning from) her own mistakes rather than always being told what to do, and so she thinks that is the best way to raise kids. The husband grew up with a much clearer sense that children should obey their parents, and he holds this as an important biblical value. They talk about it for quite some time but continue to parent in different ways, in a manner which is confusing for the children. Eventually, without being overbearing, and having asked other friends to counsel them and pray with them, the husband gently says, "We can't really carry on like this—it's not fair on the kids. I am asking, for the first time in our marriage in something significant, that you follow me on this, even though you are not persuaded. I would like to make a start by being consistent on telling the kids to use 'Mum' and 'Dad' rather than 'Bob' and 'Mary'" (names have been changed).

In both those (real-life) instances, I think that the husband is gently, sacrificially, thoughtfully leading in his marriage.

## NOURISHING AND PROVIDING

Husbands are to spiritually nourish their wives and their children. The same word is used of the husband's activity in relation to both his wife and his children in Ephesians 5 and 6:

*No one ever hated his own flesh but **nourishes** and cherishes it. (Ephesians 5:29, ESV)*

*Fathers ... bring them up [literally, **nourish** them] in the discipline and instruction of the Lord. (6:4, ESV)*

This is the same word that Paul uses to describe his ministry among the Thessalonians: he nourished them with the gospel (1 Thessalonians 2:7). Paul calls the husband and dad to take a lead in nourishing his family spiritually.

It is manly to know your Bible well. It's manly to nourish your family with the Bible, whether that is your immediate family or the wider church family (like Paul did). I'm not saying you need a theological degree—but you are called to cultivate an appetite to grow as a Christian and to model a life of prayer and time spent in the Bible, making sure, as far as you're able, that your whole family are feeding on God's word. I think a lot of Christian teenagers would testify that they can't remember a single family devotion time, but they can remember that their dad made sure it happened. It was important to him—just as important as school grades and his own work (indeed, more important).

It is also manly to ensure that your family is nourished by being committed to a church. A godly man will ensure that his family receive solid biblical food at church and that the children's and youth work is not just entertainment but also teaches the Scriptures and helps equip kids for living godly lives in our secular culture.

I'm sometimes asked, "In a marriage, should the man's vocation always come first?" I want to give a nuanced answer to this question: I think the kingdom of God comes first, and a good husband will take decisions to help the family serve the kingdom of God.

The Bible does seem to suggest that there are slightly different centres of gravity for men and women. There is something of an outward-facing focus for men and a nurturing-focus for women. In Genesis 2, the man is made from the ground to work the ground[23] whereas the woman is made from his side to help him. As we observed at the start of this chapter, when the curse comes in Genesis 3, it is his work but her labour for the family that are cursed. In 1 Timothy, there appears to be a slightly different leaning in what a husband and a wife will manage:

*He [the overseer] must **manage** his own family well and see that his children obey him, and he must do so in a manner worthy of full respect. (1 Timothy 3:4)*

*The elders who direct [literally **manage**] the affairs of the church well are worthy of double honour. (5:17)*

---

23 In Hebrew there is a lovely resonance, as Adam is made from *adamah* (the ground).

*So I counsel younger widows to marry, to have children, to* **manage** *their homes and to give the enemy no opportunity for slander. (5:14)*[24]

Both the men and women are leaders, in different spheres. He is more outward-facing while she is more inward-facing. There is a similar inward/outward dynamic in Proverbs 31, although here the wife of noble character manages a business, makes the money and runs the home. This enables the husband to be managing the town as a leader at the city gate.

Proverbs 31 should be a caution not to caricature who should be doing what. I don't think it's necessarily true to say that a marriage will struggle if a wife earns more than her husband, due to the financial dynamics this creates. That suggests a somewhat insecure husband, and biblically, the value of work is not determined by salary but by its service to God and to others.

The wise husband will take responsibility to think about and discuss with his wife how best to use the respective gifts that they have to serve the kingdom of God. The precise form that takes will depend upon the respective skills, strengths and opportunities that they have each been given.

---

24 The Greek word used in this verse is actually different from 3:4 and 5:17. In those two verses, the verb is *proistemi* (direct; stand before; lead). In 5:14 the noun is *oikodespotes*: ruler of the house. The word in 5:14 is used of the God/landowner figure in the parable of the wicked tenants (Matthew 21:33-46).

## RESPONSIBILITY OUTSIDE OF MARRIAGE

If you're not married, thanks for getting to this point in the chapter. What does all this look like outside of marriage?

To be clear, I do not think Genesis 2 or any other text suggests that all women should submit to all men—in society or in the church—because the leadership spoken of here is for within the loving commitment of marriage, where a man has promised to specifically and sacrificially love his wife. Yet at the same time, it would be strange if single men did not prepare for this in some way. I think we should expect some echo of this taking of responsibility in all manhood; otherwise we may be suggesting that a boy can only become fully a man if he marries. Biblically, being able to spiritually lead is a mark of mature masculinity. There are lots of different ways of leading (don't be constrained by the examples you've seen); and to offer some Christian leadership should be something we all, as men, aspire to.

In 1 Timothy 3, Paul lists certain qualities that *must* be seen in someone who is going to be a church leader. Yet all these are also simply marks of Christian maturity that *all* of us should aspire to:

*Now the overseer is to be above reproach, faithful to his wife, temperate, self-controlled, respectable, hospitable, able to teach, not given to drunkenness, not violent but gentle, not quarrelsome, not a lover of money. He must manage his own family well and see that his children obey him, and he must do so in a manner worthy of full respect.*

*(If anyone does not know how to manage his own family, how can he take care of God's church?) (1 Timothy 3:2-5)*

With the exception of "able to teach", Paul is simply describing mature believers. We could go through this entire list profitably. It would certainly be one conclusion to the sentence we're completing:

*To be a godly man means... to be above reproach, self-controlled, temperate... and so on.*

Yet for our purpose in this chapter, the point is that before someone can lead in the church, they must demonstrate leadership. For single men, this can be demonstrated in leading small groups or in managing volunteers, or just generally in how they relate to others. We should want to be men who take a lead and are able to offer direction, and who do so with gentleness and in the interests of others. This means we will expect, as men, to be aspiring to show some gentle and appropriate leadership outside of the formal roles of husband or overseer.[25]

This informal leadership cannot be demanded. It can only ever be offered. But, for example, if a group of single men and women were going on holiday together, I would think it appropriate for a single guy to suggest they read a Christian book during the week or to suggest that one

25 If we do not think that single men should be demonstrating a gentle leadership and a willingness to shoulder responsibility, then we must be saying that it is impossible for a single man to be an elder. I don't know anyone who thinks that!

evening they take time to pray for one another. I don't mean in an insistent, demanding way, or in a way that claims, "I'm in charge". Yet there is surely some fittingness to this sort of behaviour when single, as preparation for offering a gentle spiritual lead as a husband or an overseer in a church.

There will be some way you can offer this kind of servant-hearted, gentle leadership outside a context of marriage or church leadership. It might be in organising an informal prayer meeting in your workplace, or getting a group together to do some street evangelism, or encouraging a Christian brother or sister to be less flaky and more committed at church. There is no official role in these cases—you are just offering to gently take a lead.

At this point you may think, "But by temperament I am a natural follower". Remember, temperament is not the crucial aspect here—husbands are to take gentle responsibility regardless of their own personality. All of us are followers in some settings but should probably be offering a lead in others.

> To be a godly man means... taking responsibility to provide sacrificial leadership in a fashion appropriate to the roles and relationships I find myself in.

Which means asking yourself: what should that currently look like in the different relationships that I'm in?

# PRINCIPLE #3
# BE AMBITIOUS FOR GOD

Maleambition.com is nothing if not confident. Its front page promises that you can…

> *"Become the Alpha Male that everyone admires and women can't resist … Men want to succeed not just at their jobs but also with women, with money, with prestige, with power."*

It offers plenty of video content, broken down into four categories: attraction, grooming, manhood and physique.

What do you make of that? You might find it appalling. You might quietly think it's quite appealing. And actually there is something right and appropriate about being ambitious to achieve something in life; it is good to be worthy of admiration. *In general* (yes, I'm still saying that), men do like to achieve things. Our ambitions will vary in size, but there's a reason men like "Tough Mudders" or "Munro bagging" (slightly grandiose titles for "endurance courses involving crawling through mud" and "climbing hills"). We're built to be ambitious—to strive to succeed.

The problem with maleambition's sales pitch to men is not that it's ambitious but that what it's ambitious for feels horribly self-centred—it is presented as success in the service of you rather than of others. That can't be right for the Christian.

It's not wrong to be ambitious. The issue is what we're ambitious for. The godly man channels his ambition to achieve and puts it in God's service.

Christians follow a man who had huge ambition. Jesus came to save the world! It's his example that should shape our ambitions and model to us what godly ambition looks like. He did all that he did in the service of others. He was a compelling leader that others wanted to follow (Luke 5:11), and yet he always acted with compassion and had time for the marginalised (7:11-15). He was utterly resolute in staying on his mission (4:43; 9:51), even at huge personal cost (22:44). He was a compelling figure to the down-and-outs as well as to the rich and powerful (18:38; 19:3).

He achieved more than you and I will ever do. If we want to be ambitious—and ambition is a good thing—let's look at him.

### AMBITION: GODLY OR SELFISH?
There are, then, godly ambitions:

> It has always been my ambition to preach the gospel where Christ was not known. (Romans 15:20)

*Make it your ambition to lead a quiet life: you should mind your own business and work with your hands, just as we told you, so that your daily life may win the respect of outsiders and so that you will not be dependent on anybody. (1 Thessalonians 4:11)*

Paul wanted to preach the gospel where no one else had been. It was a magnificent obsession that drove his life. Not all of us will have that obsession to serve the Lord by reaching the unreached (though you might), and Paul knew that. His instruction to the Thessalonians was more modest—get a job and do it properly so that you're not financially dependent on others and so that non-Christians respect how you live. Paul was always concerned with the reputation of the gospel.

But there are selfish ambitions too—aims that serve to raise our profile, win us some glory, feather our nest or improve our reputation. This kind of ambition crops up several times in lists of vices (2 Corinthians 12:20; Galatians 5:20; Philippians 1:17; James 3:14, 16). Philippians 2:3 mentions selfish ambition too, and offers a helpful contrast:

*Do nothing out of selfish ambition or vain conceit. Rather, in humility value others above yourselves.*

Paul challenges our *motives*: why we work, why we pursue money, why we take up leadership. We are not to be driven by ambition for self but for others.

## SIDENOTE: PHYSICAL AMBITIONS

I'm going to spend most of this chapter thinking about types of work, but first I want to step sideways a little. One of the things I found striking on maleambition. com is how much attention is given to male grooming and physique. When I was a teenager (admittedly over three decades ago), the most exotic male-grooming product we might have bought was a pot of hair gel (of the sort of rough texture that nowadays would only get used by a builder to attach tiles). Since then, the male grooming/beauty industry has gone crazy. In 2021 the total globally spent on male grooming products was just short of $31 billion. In the UK men spent £73.8 million on our faces, and in the US $3.2 billion.[26] (I'd argue the difference is because British men are more handsome. I might be biased.)

Apparently, it all changed in the nineties. That's when magazines like *Men's Health* started to publish photos of unbelievably muscular guys (literally unbelievable in part, because of air-brushing) and articles focusing on achieving the perfect set of abs. (Growing up I think I had no idea what abs were—now there are currently 52.7 million posts on the #abs Instagram feed).

I'm not suggesting that godly men ought to look like Jabba the Hutt in *Star Wars*, with wrinkled skin and saggy everything else. Going to the gym is a very healthy stress

---

26 https://www.statista.com/topics/3995/men-s-grooming-and-cosmetics-
market-in-europe/#topicHeader__wrapper (accessed November 28, 2022).

release for some and a bonding activity with friends for others. I'm simply observing that, compared to the rest of history, our culture is remarkably concerned with physical ambitions. I can't help but wonder whether in eternity we'll care a whole lot less about times achieved on Strava, PBs in the gym and what we can "bench". Beware making a good hobby into a selfish ambition. It's worth asking the question of whether you're tempted, or how you're tempted, to do that.

## WHAT DO YOU WANT TO BE?

Did you have a clear idea as a child of what you wanted to be (astronaut, fireman, sportsman, world king)? Personally, I can't remember any clear sense of occupation I desired. I may simply have been spectacularly unimaginative or unambitious. I'm a little clearer these days about what I want to be. I'm also far clearer about how much influence I have on what I'll become—a lot!

The decisions I make today will determine who I am tomorrow. That's true at a banal level: what I eat and drink tonight will affect how I relate to others in the morning. Yet at a more profound level, in our very being we know that there is truth in the saying, "Sow a thought, reap an action; sow an action, reap a habit; sow a habit, reap a character; sow a character, reap a destiny."

Most of us will not be able to decide to become a professional sportsman; we exist with physiological limits. We can't all resolve to become a world-class composer; some innate talent is required. But we *can* plan to serve the Lord wholeheartedly and make the most of what he has given us. We *can* resolve to become more like Jesus, and we have a massive influence on whether we can achieve that. We *can* decide today what sort of character we want to be tomorrow.

To put it in a simple equation:

Ambition + activity = achievement

"It's too late for that," say some of you. "I'm already grown up; I won't change now." That's only true if you decide it's true. In the West, even at the point of retirement, most of us will still have roughly a quarter of our adult lives left. That's 25% of your lifetime to be useful in God's service and ambitious for him.[27] And when you're retired, you don't even have work to distract you from godly ambition! No one sensible rejects a quarter of their savings. No one reasonable abandons their holiday when there's 25% of it left.

Only a fool would permanently give up a quarter of their sleep each night. Don't give up on a quarter of your adult life. (And for most reading this, we'll have a lot more than that still to go).

---

27 If you've looked this one up, there's an element of pedantry in your character. Adulthood begins at 18 and the average age of male death is 81 (82.9 Australia, 81.2 UK, 78.79 USA)—so we have an adulthood of 62 years. If you retire aged 65, you have 16 out of 63 years left.

## JUST WALK

The godly man is ambitious to grow a character like Jesus. It's not enough to desire to grow your character; you have to make choices and take decisions to actually do so. In biblical language, we need to be deliberate about what paths we are walking on. That's a metaphor that runs throughout the Bible, but it comes with greatest frequency and density in the book of Proverbs—for instance:

> *I instruct you in the way of wisdom and lead you along straight paths. When you walk, your steps will not be hampered; when you run, you will not stumble. Hold on to instruction, do not let it go; guard it well, for it is your life. Do not set foot on the path of the wicked or walk in the way of evildoers. (Proverbs 4:11-14)*

Walking is such a great metaphor; we all understand it, regardless of where we live. Any one step doesn't achieve a lot, but repeated steps in the same direction can take you a long way. My wife and I are on a ten-year project to walk all 630 miles of the South West coast path in the UK, taking a week each year to try and knock off 60-75 miles. (We're a third done, if you're interested.) Most of it is absolutely stunning, but it's pretty up and down as you climb a hill, then descend into a cove, then walk along a beach, and repeat. Often one of us will suggest, "Shall we have a rest?" to which the now-standard response is "Let's see where we are in 15 more minutes". It's amazing how far you can walk in a mere 15 minutes. You just put one foot in front of the other, and you're no longer where you were.

You'd be forgiven for saying, "Matt, I have grasped the concept of walking". Yet Proverbs goes on and on about it, because clearly we don't get the concept when it comes to character! We have to be deliberate. We have to choose what we think about and what we do. We're choosing today who we will be tomorrow.

So, what path are you walking on?

Where is your thought life taking you?

Who are your actions turning you into?

There's no neutral. You can't say, "I'm not walking anywhere". That simply means your life is going nowhere—which is still a destination, but just not one you want to reach. A while back, someone sent me a quote from an old American poet, James Terry White:

> "It is not necessary for a man to be actively bad in order to make a failure in life; simple inaction will accomplish it …
> It is the constant effort to get higher and further which develops manhood and character."

Maybe it feels like you're doing nothing wrong—but that's because you're not doing much at all. Of course walking nowhere is better than walking into danger. But you're still going nowhere!

Make sure you walk on wise paths. Choose today who you want to be tomorrow. Be ambitious to be more and more like Jesus.

## AMBITIOUS IN YOUR WORK

For the rest of this chapter, we'll focus on our work. After his creation, it's the first thing the first man is given to do:

> The LORD God took the man and put him in the Garden of Eden to **work it** and **guard it**.
>
> *(Genesis 2:15, my translation, emphasis added)*

We'll look at "guarding" in the next chapter—here we're thinking about our work (or, as the word could be translated, our service). We are given the task of building things—of achieving things of value. Of course, the woman is given to work too, but the man takes the lead in the garden.

At this point, most of us can feel positive. If you're doing useful work of any kind, in a paid or volunteer capacity, then that is a manly activity. Let's think about that under a couple of very broad categories.

## PRODUCTIVE WORK

Many cultures around the world have a rite of passage into manhood.

In Vanuatu, boys climb a tower 30 metres (98 feet) high and jump off with nothing but a vine tied around their legs. The objective is to touch the ground without breaking your neck. If you do so, you are now officially a man.

In the Amazonian Mawé tribe, a boy is required to stick his hand into a glove filled with bullet ants. (In case you're wondering, they're called bullet ants because they have the most painful sting of any insect—it is like being hit by a bullet.) Once a boy has endured this wildly painful sting (which is also excruciating in duration), he is then a man.

Meanwhile, in most of the developed West, to transition from boy to man you need to... get a job.

There is something biblically appropriate about that cultural reference point. We are made to work. Work forces you to take responsibility, ensures that you don't waste your time, and teaches you how to relate to others you may not like or who are really quite difficult. It enables you to develop new skills. Work is good. God has given to us the task of taking the raw materials of the earth and using them to help others.

Gardeners take seeds and arrange them in the ground to produce crops. Lawyers take words and arrange them in a document to protect clients. Factory workers take components and make cars. Teachers take information and communicate it simply to produce educated pupils. Refuse collectors take away rubbish and keep streets clean. Musicians take notes and arrange them on a page to produce music.

Productive work is good. Idleness kills manliness.

I referred back in the introduction to Jordan Peterson's work. In thinking about masculinity, I've read and listened to some of his material because he clearly connects with lots of young men. In the end, I think his message is simple: men need a purpose and they need to take responsibility. That's what helps them. While this might sound obvious, he says it *really clearly,* and a lot of guys have testified that it's a message that has pulled them out of despair.

Bible readers should find this utterly unsurprising. We said in the last chapter that taking responsibility (in an appropriate way) was inherent to masculinity. So is working. "One who is slack in his work is brother to one who destroys" (Proverbs 18:9).

I called this section "productive" work rather than simply "paid" work. Sometimes work dries up. Sometimes, in a recession, a lot of people lose their jobs. But you don't become less of a man if you're unemployed. However, you do need to find something useful to do, whether that's home improvement, giving a lot more time to church, or helping out at a youth club. We need to know that we are doing something useful and productive. Lounging around playing games or watching TV is fun for a while, but it cannot be a way of life, and it will never really satisfy.

As others have said, while some are idle when it comes to work, for others work becomes an idol. We men can find it hard to pull apart who we are from what we do. Many of us have a subconscious ranking of jobs in our heads, and we value some people more highly simply because of what their profession or job title is. We need to be frequently told that we're not defined by our jobs but by the Lord.

How can you know if your work is becoming an idol? Ask yourself:

*Am I more ambitious for promotion and higher pay than I am to become more like Jesus?*

*Do I spend more time thinking about and worrying about my work and my career than I do the eternal fate of my family and friends?*

I know what the answers are meant to be, but the questions are unsettling.

We need to know that our jobs will pass. My father was never a high-flyer at work. My parents lived in farming country, and he sold fuel to farmers for most of his life. He was good at it—he had customers who were loyal to him over decades because they knew he went the extra mile for them. The upshot was that, for him, doing business often consisted of popping in to have coffee with a friend and collecting an order for tractor fuel or lubricants. It seemed to me like he did quite well at easing out of work. Aged 65, he dropped to three days a week; then at 70 he went down to a couple of days a week. I remember being out for a walk with him one day when his mobile rang and he took an order. I asked him, "Dad, why don't you just stop work all together?" His reply: "I'm not ready for the phone to stop ringing."

Within a year or so, though, he realised that he was ready and was quite content with his garden, his lawn bowls and his family. But others never quite make the transition. The phone stops ringing, the emails stop arriving and they look up and have... nothing. That's because they have made their work their everything. And the problem is that, through retirement or, erm, the ultimate "retirement", your work, with all the hopes and ambitions and worries and successes that went with it, will pass.

So the question becomes: what is it that you're doing which will last?

## ETERNAL WORK

During the course of my life, I've had plenty of obsessions and ambitions, some of them more useful than others. In no obvious ranking order, I think of...

- Completing a football sticker album. (Ambition realised early on in life.)

- Reaching the end of Manic Miner, a computer game from the 1980s. (The only computer game I completed. Don't look it up, it's horribly dated.)

- Becoming a cool teenager. (Pretty sure I never achieved that.)

- Achieving a first-class degree (Failed... but due to my insecurities, I feel the need to say that this was because I spent the final term in hospital.)

- Learning Hebrew verbs. (I sort of did, but it was a long while ago now, and I have forgotten a good chunk of them.)

- ~~Owning a bigger house, a garden, a garage to store things in.~~ (I'm a Christian minister so shouldn't admit that there are times when I really do desire these things.)

- Having a larger family.

- Leading a larger church, where lots of people become Christians and plenty serve as missionaries to unreached people groups.

- Reaching the end of my life serving Christ faithfully.

A pretty mixed list, overall (though on my harder days, I can always fall back on having completed Manic Miner). What would you write, if you were composing a list of your past aspirations? And which of them will last into eternity? This leads us to the second broad category—the work of the Lord: "Give yourself fully to the work of the Lord, because you know that your labour in the Lord is not in vain" (1 Corinthians 15:58).

In the context of the past resurrection of Jesus and the future resurrection of his people, Paul encourages us with the truth that work we have done to advance the gospel among unbelievers and to establish believers in Christ will endure into eternity; it is not in vain. It will not pass. All productive work is valuable and pleasing to the Lord, and work done in a godly manner serves him (Colossians 3:23-24), but Paul is talking specifically in 1 Corinthians about the ministry of evangelising non-Christians and of building up Christians. That's what the "work of the Lord" is throughout the letter (3:9-15; 16:10; 16:15-16).[28]

It doesn't matter whether you are a gardener, poet, hairdresser or accountant; the Lord will reward you for faithfully carrying out your work. Yet we are not told that we will take our gardens, poems, haircuts and sums into the new creation. It is the "work of the Lord" that lasts into eternity—and this must affect our ambitions. I know that at 10:30 on a Tuesday morning, it's what your employer requires that consumes your thoughts, not "the work of the Lord". I know that most of us have paid work to do. But that cannot be the limit of our ambitions. Only the work of the Lord lasts. So, as well as (actually, more than) the desire to complete an Ironman or to achieve a certain position in our career, we should be ambitious about the work of the Lord. And we can do that work of building up believers and sharing the gospel in our street, in our families, in our churches, in our offices, and in those we do our hobbies with or play sport with.

---

28 I found an article by Peter Orr particularly persuasive on this point: "Abounding in the Work of the Lord: 1 Cor 15:58" in *Themelios 38.2*, 2013, p 205-214.

My father was not a Christian man. He was often deeply resistant to discussing the Christian faith. In honest moments he would tell me, "I don't want to be told that I've wasted time on things in this life that don't matter".

I'd normally reply, "It's not that they don't matter, Dad—you've brought yourself and many others pleasure through gardening; it's a good gift that you've enjoyed. But it will not last." And it hasn't. My parents' house was sold when they died, and the last time I drove past, the garden that was once the envy of the village was a complete mess.

For myself, I don't know how many of my present or past ambitions and obsessions are noble or at least useful ones, but there's one ambition I pursued and I'll never regret. Despite my father's anger and hostility to the gospel, I did just about persist in trying to talk to him about Jesus. And not long before he died in his eighties, he trusted Jesus to take him to heaven.

The ambition to see him in eternity was probably the one obsession that I am most pleased that I had, because, even though I miss him greatly, I will see him again. The work of the Lord is never in vain.

*To be a godly man means… being ambitious for God.* Perhaps you need to be more ambitious than you are. Perhaps you need to be ambitious for different things than you are. If someone looked at how you spend your weeks, would they say "That guy is an ambitious guy"? The answer should be "Yes". And what would they say you're ambitious for? The answer should be "To serve like Jesus". To become like Jesus. To work productively. To do the work of the Lord. The world may not particularly praise that guy. But God will.

# PRINCIPLE #4
# USE YOUR STRENGTH TO PROTECT

"To do the right thing, you might have to die."[29]

That was a headline after the horrific shooting at Robb Elementary School in Uvalde, Texas in 2022. The shooting produced what some called a "unity in fury" among Americans, who were angry that police officers waited outside the school for an hour and fifteen minutes before entering. During that time 19 children and two teachers were killed. The author quoted from the police training manual that the officers were meant to follow:

*"First responders to the active shooter scene will usually be required to place themselves in harm's way and display uncommon acts of courage to save the innocent."*

They were meant to fight to protect the children, even if that meant placing themselves in harm's way. They were meant to act with courage. It would undoubtedly

---

29 https://frenchpress.thedispatch.com/p/to-do-the-right-thing-you-might-have (accessed November 28, 2022).

have been tragic if police officers had died in saving the lives of children, yet amid that grief, they would have been revered as heroes. Rather than provoking outrage, they would have been rightly lauded for their sacrifice—because it takes courage to fight and defend others.

I can't honestly say what I would have done if I had been a police officer outside the school that day, but I know what I *should* have done. Sacrificing your life to protect others is in line with the biblical pattern that a part of masculinity is to be prepared to die to guard and protect the church, the truth, and the lives of others.

In his wisdom, God created men as protectors. We're going to take two chapters to think about using male strength to protect. In this chapter, we'll look at protecting the truth in and of the church. In the next chapter, we'll explore the more general sense of how we have a duty to protect women—in particular our spiritual sisters, mothers and daughters.

## GUARDING THE HOUSE

We noted in the previous chapter that in Genesis 2 the first man was given two key tasks before the woman was created:

> *The LORD God took the man and put him in the Garden of Eden to **work it** and **guard it**.*
>
> *(Genesis 2:15, emphasis added)*

These same two verbs are used later in the Old Testament to describe the work of the male levitical priests in the tabernacle, the tent within which God dwelled among his people (my translation, emphasis added):

*They are to **guard** all the furnishings of the tent of meeting, fulfilling the obligations of the Israelites by doing the **work** of the tabernacle. (Numbers 3:8)*

*Only you and your sons may **guard** as priests in connection with everything at the altar and inside the curtain. I am giving you the **work** of the priesthood.*
*(Numbers 18:7)*

*The Levites were to **guard** the tent of meeting and the sanctuary and to attend the sons of Aaron, their brothers for the **work** of the house of the LORD.*
*(1 Chronicles 23:32)*

*And I will appoint them to **guard** the temple, for all the **work** that is to be done in it. (Ezekiel 44:14)*

As Bible scholars have pointed out, these echoes are strongly suggestive that the first man was placed in the Garden of Eden as a priest to guard and protect the dwelling place of God.[30] Adam was not only meant to make the garden fruitful; he was meant to keep it safe. That's a central activity for the first man—offering protection to the garden and therefore also to the woman in the garden

---

30 I think I first encountered the idea in Greg Beale, *The Temple and the Church's Mission* (Apollos, 2004), especially p 66-75, which highlights the garden as the place of the first priest, the first guarding cherubim and the first tree (which was reflected in the temple furnishings by the tree-like lampstand).

(all of which makes the events of Genesis 3, where he fails to do so, all the more tragic). Lots of police forces have adopted the slogan "To protect and to serve". It's a good one. You might ask how well it is lived out, but it's still a great job description. Genesis 2:15 suggests it's also a pretty good job description for any man.

At the risk of a little controversy, I would suggest that occasionally this role as a guardian requires some aggressive force. That is obvious in the case of police officers (including those in Uvalde, who eventually shot dead the gunman who was attacking school children). Violence towards the wicked is required in order to provide protection to the innocent. So we shouldn't be surprised that we see that same model in the Bible. God himself is described as a warrior who fights to protect his people (for example, Exodus 15:3; Isaiah 42:13).[31] At points, being the guardian of God's house and his truth requires a little aggression.

We see this kind of protective, measured aggression in Moses breaking the tablets of the covenant and the violent destruction of the golden calf in Exodus 32. Moses had only been up Mount Sinai for 40 days, yet Israel had rebelled and demanded fresh gods from Aaron, who made them the calf to worship. When Moses came down the mountain, he smashed the two stone tablets of the covenant, destroyed the golden calf and ordered the Levites to kill all those who continued to rebel. That last action is more shocking.

---

31 Even more common is the title "Lord of Hosts" (or "Armies").

But what was Moses doing? He was removing a cancer of rebellion in order to save the body of the nation of Israel. In his godly zeal, Moses realised that some violence was required in order to protect the people from their sin and save the overwhelming majority of the nation.

Along the same lines is what happens in Numbers 25, when an Israelite man brings a Midianite (read: not part of God's people, living in rebellion against God) back to the camp to have sex with her. Phinehas, Aaron's grandson, kills them with a spear. Phinehas knew that Israel's rebellion and worship of Baal, the Midianite god, had brought a plague which had killed 24,000 of them— and here was this man, rejecting God and his commands in the midst of the people of God. His violent action was designed as a precise, measured strike to remove the problem and save the nation. His actions demonstrated a zeal for the honour of the Lord and also made atonement for the Israelites' sin.

To be clear, these are not *physically* models for us to follow today! That was the mistake of medieval Crusaders and that is the mistake of some unacceptably violent Christian protests in our day. Nowhere is such physical aggression commended in the New Testament—and when Peter drew a sword to protect Jesus when he was about to be arrested, the Lord told him to sheath it rather than use it (John 18:10-11). Church discipline is the equivalent, reluctant action in the New Testament. If appeals for repentance have been rejected, church leaders defend their congregations by shutting out those who are behaving sinfully and unapologetically (for instance, in ongoing scandalous sin, 1 Corinthians 5:1-2; in false teaching, Galatians 1:6-9; or in being divisive, Titus 3:9-11).

This zeal to protect and guard, this passion to keep God's people safe, this willingness to be unpopular in order to protect God's name, his truth and his people—these are virtues associated with the male priesthood in the Old Testament and church leaders in the New.

## WHAT MAKES A GOOD SHEPHERD?

Most of us will be familiar with Jesus calling himself the good shepherd, and David (of Goliath-slaying fame) having worked as a shepherd before he was called to serve as king of Israel. What, fundamentally, is a shepherd's task? It is to be a protector. David did not stop being a shepherd when he became the king—he just swapped sheep for people. Shepherding is a metaphor that emerges in the Old Testament and continues into the New.

While it is chiefly the kings of Israel who were called to be shepherds, the prophets broadened this out to the religious leadership more generally.[32] When they fail, the Lord says that he himself will come and reveal how shepherds should behave: namely, with tenderness and

---

32 Numbers 27:17—Moses and Aaron were the original shepherds, but the term seems chiefly to refer to kings of God's people in the Old Testament.

with strength so that they care for the sheep and fight off threats to the sheep:

- He gathers the lambs in his arms *and* he rules with a mighty arm. (Isaiah 40:10-11)

- He rescues the lost, binds up the wounds of the broken *and* destroys those who have exploited his people. (Ezekiel 34:16)

- He saves those who are pushed away *and* he judges those who are bullies. (Ezekiel 34:20-22)

Here is a remarkable combination of tenderness and fierceness. We see it at times in the Old Testament: the destruction of the prophets of Baal in 1 Kings 18 and then the tender provision of food and drink for the broken Elijah afterwards; the judgment of God in famine upon the wickedness of Israel and yet his tender kindness towards Ruth and Naomi in the book of Ruth. Yet these are mere glimpses compared to the clarity with which we see these shepherding Scriptures fulfilled in the New Testament. When Jesus comes, he reveals himself as *the* good shepherd (John 10:11, 14). He protects his sheep from robbers and from wolves (v 1-5, 11-12). He lays down his life for the sheep (v 11). He knows his sheep, and his sheep know him (v 14). No one can take the life of this strong shepherd (v 18), and no one can snatch any of his sheep out of his hand (v 28).

Shepherds put their lives on the line. Their job was to enter into combat with robbers and with wolves. Jesus showed that the failure of the shepherds of God's people to do their job was contemptible (v 12-13). And while he is *the* good shepherd, in his word he calls men to act as under-shepherds to his sheep—to protect the people of God (1 Peter 5:1-2).

## TOUGH AND TENDER

Let's return to one of the verses summarised above: God gathers the lambs in his arms *and* he rules with a mighty arm (Isaiah 40:10-11).

It's a striking image. The arms of God are used for both tender gathering and tough, musclebound ruling. I imagine that most of us men lean in one direction by temperament—either defaulting to aggression or sympathy. However, as the uniquely perfect man, Jesus knew precisely when to confront and rebuke religious leaders and rage at those defiling the temple courts; he also knew exactly when to welcome children into his arms and when to be tender with women broken by sinful mistakes and society's stigma.

See him scatter the money-changers in the temple by cracking a whip and overturning tables, and then see him speak with a Samaritan woman of dubious repute so that she is persuaded that he is the Saviour of the world (John 2:13-17; 4:1-42). See him struck to the heart at the grief of a widow burying her only son, and then resurrecting him so that, in words of understated simplicity, "Jesus gave him back to his mother"; and then see him rebuke the crowd for their fickleness in religious matters and unwillingness to follow him (Luke 7:11-16, 31-35).

This combination of toughness and tenderness is what we want from our leaders. It's also what we should aspire to ourselves. It's what kids want from their dads.

I enjoyed a little exchange I had with a couple of four-year-old boys at church recently. One declared to me (with no context whatsoever), "Matt, did you know that my dad is so strong, he can jump right over a house?" The other boy looked a little wounded, before replying, "But my dad is so strong, he can lift up two houses at once—one on each arm!"

When their dads wandered over and I mentioned this exchange, the inclination of both boys was to hug their dad's legs. These boys wanted to be hugged and loved by their dads, and they wanted the reassurance that their dads were strong enough to protect them. They wanted to know their dads were both tough *and* tender.

It's foolish to take our own temperament and project that (or its opposite) onto masculinity. One guy might shout, "Real men fight" while another says, "Real men display gentleness". By contrast, the godly man knows his own temperament and recognises its strengths, but at the same time he knows that sometimes he needs to ignore his default setting and act the other way.

I'm reminded of one time in my early twenties when an older man said to me, "Matt, you have the most wonderful zeal for the truth. It really is commendable. Now, if you could just combine that zeal with love for people, then you might possibly do some good rather than relational damage."

That hurt. But he was right. I needed to learn to be tender, not just tough—gentle as well as right. I remain grateful to that older man telling that younger version of me how to grow up to be a more helpful shepherding man—for telling me what biblical masculinity looks like.

## PROTECTING SHEEP

God requires godly men to step up to be the shepherds of God's people. It is unsurprising in the New Testament that those responsible for the authoritative teaching that protects the church are to be appropriately qualified men. The role of protector is a part of what it means to be male.

Paul tells the elders of the church in Ephesus:

> Be shepherds of the church of God, which he bought with his own blood. I know that after I leave, savage wolves will come in among you and will not spare the flock.
>
> (Acts 20:28)

Protecting others from spiritual wolves... that's acting a lot like Jesus! It's manly to fight to protect the church and its doctrine. Of course, the manner of doing so is not with violence but with prayer and godliness, and in gracious debate:

*I want the men everywhere to pray, lifting up holy hands
without anger or disputing. (1 Timothy 2:8)*

*But you, man of God, flee from all this, and pursue
righteousness, godliness, faith, love, endurance and
gentleness. Fight the good fight of the faith.*
*(1 Timothy 6:11-12)*

*The weapons we fight with are not the weapons of the
world ... We demolish arguments and every pretension
that sets itself up against the knowledge of God, and we
take captive every thought to make it obedient to Christ.*
*(2 Corinthians 10:4-5)*

Prayer, godliness and engaging in debate are all hard
work! Some of us may be strong in one department but
weak in the others. We need them all, and we need to
display them biblically and not in a worldly fashion. We
need to channel our capacity for aggression (whether
verbal or physical) in the right way.

The New Testament is well aware that, when provoked,
men can be quick to lift their hands in anger (1 Timothy
2:8). The godly contrast is to lift hands in prayer. The
context in that chapter is that there is a world that
needs to know about Jesus, the one mediator between
God and humanity—but there are false teachers leading
people away from him. That should make us men
angry. That should make us want to fight—but not
with our hands but with prayer. Not with angry fingers
slapping a keyboard to write ungodly, uncharitable
posts, but with kindness and gentle instruction

2 Timothy 2:24-25). Again, it's worth asking, "Does my character default to toughness or tenderness? Am I someone who loves fights, or am I someone who always finds a reason to avoid them?"

The task given to appropriate men to be guardians of God's household means that when we turn to a passage such as 1 Timothy 2:11-15, we should be entirely unsurprised that the ministry of delivering the authoritative teaching in a church is given to suitably qualified men:

> *A woman should learn in quietness and full submission. I do not permit a woman to teach or to assume authority over a man; she must be quiet. For Adam was formed first, then Eve. And Adam was not the one deceived; it was the woman who was deceived and became a sinner.*
> *(1 Timothy 2:11)*

These verses need some serious study—and I'm not doing that here![33] For our purposes, though, we can make the following observations:

- The word "quiet" is a relational one. It doesn't mean "silent" but rather "respectful, or "not disruptive". (Notice that all Christians are to be "quiet" in relationship to their government in v 2.)

---

33 If you'd like to think about this passage in more detail, I'd recommend Andreas Köstenberger and Thomas Schreiner, *Women in the Church: An Analysis and Application of 1 Timothy 2:9-15* (Baker Academic, 2005).

- In the pastoral epistles, "teaching" seems to chiefly be a reference to the authoritative passing on of a body of Christian truth (see 4:13; 6:2b; 2 Timothy 1:13-14); and it's this task that falls to the male elders (1 Timothy 3:2; 5:17).

- The women in the congregation are not to take on the role of authoritative Bible teaching[34]; that falls to the qualified male elders.

- The reason given is that Adam was formed first (and so was responsible for the task of guarding God's garden dwelling-place). When that allocation of roles is rejected, then the chaos of 2:14 ensues.[35]

The simple point is that the guardians responsible for authoritative teaching are suitably qualified male elders. That is entirely consistent with the rest of the Bible: it was male levitical priests who guarded the house of God in the Old Testament. It was male apostles who initially guarded the truth of the gospel. It is male shepherds who serve as church elders. Even at the end of history, the New

---

34 To my mind, this means the main sermon to the gathered congregation. Taking a lead in a Bible study, where anyone can interrupt and ask questions or offer a correction, is very different from a 30-minute (or however long) monologue to the whole church from one of the designated leaders.

35 It is not that Eve is being made responsible for what happened. We've already seen that Adam was responsible, and to make Eve to blame in such a way would run against Genesis 3:17 and Romans 5:14, 16.

Jerusalem is built upon the foundation of the twelve male apostles of Jesus (Revelation 21:14).

Guarding the household of God and protecting his sheep is a job for men who are qualified by their godly character and biblical doctrine. This is not to say women cannot be involved in this too, but the ultimate responsibility of protecting the church falls primarily to qualified men. This is not arbitrary and unfair—it flows fittingly from the protective role inherent to manhood. That is to say, the protective guardian role of men is not just down to their greater physical strength (in general). The Bible assumes that there is also something suitable for this role in the male temperament (in general). Those "traditional" male traits of stoicism, stubbornness and aggression are valuable in defending the truth. These traits may commonly be maligned in the West. They may be dismissed as social conditioning, though some sociologists will highlight that these traits are pretty consistent across all cultures and centuries, even when different cultures have had no contact with one another. But like all characteristics, when these traits are placed in the service of God and his people, and used according to God's commands and the Spirit's wisdom, they are positive, useful and God-honouring.

## CALLED TO CONTEND

"That's all very good," you may say, "but I'm not a church elder and have no shepherding duties". Maybe not—but remember 1 Timothy 3:1: "Whoever aspires to be an overseer desires a noble task". While there are different gifts within the household of God, it is good to aspire to the role of an overseer or elder, and qualification comes through character and resolve. As we've said already, every man should be seeking for their character and lifestyle to be like that described in 1 Timothy 3 or Titus 1, including that "he must hold firmly to the trustworthy message as it has been taught, so that he can encourage others by sound doctrine and refute those who oppose it" (Titus 1:9).

So, while not bearing the responsibility in the same way as designated elders do, all men in church should care enough about the household of God to contend for it. All Christian men should want to see God's truth and God's people protected from wolves and robbers. I can think of plenty of men in our church and others who don't currently serve as elders but who battle away in prayer, in godliness and in confronting the secular ideas of the age and taking them captive for Christ. These are tasks for every Christian man. If you are not prepared to do these, then (forgive me for being blunt) are you perhaps a little emasculated?

We need to be prepared to pay a cost for this. If you stand up in the current climate for biblical truth on gender issues or marriage issues or babies in the womb, then you'll pay a price in unpopularity, ridicule or contempt. And I can think of friends who, as lay elders in their church, took an enormous hit emotionally when they stood up to their senior pastor in order to protect the church. We need to aspire to the zeal of Phinehas in holding to sound doctrine and protecting the sheep, while using the weapons God has given to us—prayer, godliness, and gracious debate. If you think it sounds more manly to use a spear than the Bible, then you may be underestimating how much backbone it takes sometimes to stand firm and do what is best for the spiritual health of your church. No one is going to burn you at the stake, but they may ruin you online. There's a cost that will need to be paid in standing up for the truth and defending the church—but that's our role.

Two weeks after the tragedy at Robb Elementary school in Uvalde came another story. This one didn't make the international news. Jakub Szymanski was a 15-year-old boy who stepped in front of his mother to protect her from a brutal knife attack. He was rushed to hospital but died from his wounds; his mother had serious injuries but survived. The attacker was caught and is now in prison.

What instincts lead a 15-year-old to jump in front of his mother and take a knife for her? The answer, according to the Bible is this: the noble and correct reflexes that flow out of a man's duty to protect. One of Jakub's neighbours commented:

> "He was quiet, but he was a protector. He fought for his family. He was an amazing person, he was a hero and he should be remembered as one."[36]

---

36 https://bit.ly/3FBPCsb (accessed December 16, 2022).

Don't put this book down in order to go pump iron and bulk up. We've been thinking about protecting the household of God, the truth, the sheep. You're more likely to do that in a library than in a boxing ring, or in a conversation in a coffee shop rather than in the Colosseum. But it is a fight, and you're called to it. You may be quiet like Jakub, but you can be a protector. *To be a godly man means... to be ready to protect God's church.*

# PRINCIPLE #5
# DISPLAY THOUGHTFUL
# CHIVALRY

In March 2021, a 33-year-old woman called Sarah Everard went missing in central London. After several days it emerged that she had been abducted, raped and murdered by an off-duty policeman. It was a truly shocking case, and one with lasting effects. Trust in the police was severely undermined, and women felt a new wave of terror at heading out alone in the evening. It created a vast amount of comment on what men should be like and do.

I think that for a lot of men, the volume and nature of the coverage produced a realisation that Sarah's horrific death was actually on a spectrum that women navigate in public every day. It was at the very extreme end of the same spectrum as wolf whistling and harassment, both verbal and physical. It was a window into a part of the fallen world that perhaps we'd been blind to: what it's like to be a woman in a world where, on an average night out, low-level sexism is an ever-present reality and physical violation is an ever-present possibility. We need to understand that there is a reason that many women are suspicious when a man acts in an apparently kind way towards them. We must never underestimate the lasting pain of being the subject of lewd comments, hateful mockery, inappropriate touching, or worse; and we must never forget that we do not know what pain lies in the past (or present) of a woman who we work with, or sit next to on the way to work, or meet at church, and so on. Experience has taught many women to be wary of men, rather than to see them as protectors. We will have to earn trust from women generally. Men in the church need to prove themselves worthy of trust before many women can feel comfortable to grant it.

Not only that, but it is not enough to not do the wrong thing—we need to do the right thing, too. The hashtag #notallmen was trending for a while after Sarah Everard was murdered, and lots of guys were upset that they were being tarred with the same brush. *I don't wolf-whistle. I don't leer. I don't upskirt.* Yet the understandable response from women was often "You may not be guilty of this behaviour, but do you step in when you see it?" The data in London shows that harassment of women in public places such as the Underground is generally ignored. There's no reason to think that what goes for London doesn't go for other cities too. People don't like to get involved.

But what would you do if it was your sister?

## A POST-CHIVALROUS WORLD

In this chapter I want to argue that a godly man should display appropriate "chivalry". My dictionary describes this as kind behaviour, especially by men towards women—conduct which is honourable and, if needed, courageous. I know that for many of us the word suggests medieval knights, but forget them and think of it like this: chivalry is using strength to serve.

In some ways, this chapter is arguing against the grain. The word "chivalry" provokes some strong reactions. One headline I encountered asked:

*Tools of the Patriarchy: Should Chivalry Be Dead?*[37]

The writers certainly wanted chivalry to be dead. They hated the concept, as it suggests that women are physically weaker than men rather than equal. Yet (while it's unpopular to say it out loud) in general it is empirically true: on average, men are stronger than women. There is a reason why men and women do not compete together at almost every sport—it would not be equal. Men should be aware of their strength, and we should be aware that it is sometimes intimidating. We should use the strength that we have to serve, not unnerve.

And this means stepping up to protect those who are more vulnerable.

---

37 https://msmagazine.com/2020/07/30/tools-of-the-patriarchy-should-
chivalry-be-dead/ (accessed November 28, 2022).

I recently read the complaint of another young female writer:

> *"The other day I was on a run, and two men started yelling sexual remarks at me and following me. There were another two men nearby, who did nothing. If they had defended my cause, it would not be considered 'sexism', but simply 'being a considerate human'."*[38]

That seems really obvious and yet... it no longer is. What if offering help seems patronising? What if it feels "mansplainy"? Loud voices in our culture keep repeating that men are toxic and women are better off without them: "Step aside. We don't need you." I've had a young guy at church tell me that he's told a male colleague guilty of sexist banter in front of a female colleague to give it a rest, to which the woman declared, "I don't need you to stand up for me. I can do it myself." Another spoke of offering to walk a female colleague to the station late at night, only to be angrily told, "I don't need you to protect me". Others lament that they have offered their seat to a woman on the Tube and have been told, "I don't need your seat". Some speak of their paralysis over whether to hold a door open for a woman or not, having been glared at for doing so on several occasions. *We don't need you. Step aside.* As a result, lots of men do. They ignore low-level sexism.

---

38 https://threadsuk.com/conservative-or-sexist (accessed November 28, 2022).

So here's the situation. Basic consideration means stepping in. If I don't, I'm part of the problem. But stepping in might be patronising or sexist, and I'm also part of the problem. I'm not blaming anyone—frankly, women have to put up with far worse than a bit of confusion and some probably unfair annoyance. But still—it's confusing.

One surprisingly sympathetic voice is that of the feminist writer Nina Power. Her book *What Do Men Want?* complains about the post-chivalry world, where men have lost the paternal instinct to protect. She positively defines masculinity as "an abstract rage to protect". She makes (the entirely biblical) point that caring for others is not always gentle—sometimes it is fierce. Strikingly, she observes:

> "When masculine writers suggest that men should take responsibility, they are dismissed by liberal critics as 'right-wing' or worse. These attacks should be ignored if we are ever to reconfigure a form of life that permits the celebration of the beauty of sexual difference."[39]

That is a great summary of some of the truths we've been thinking about. I think that the godly guy should persist in offering to take responsibility, in making a protective gesture, in enquiring if he can help. It should be obvious that we do this at home, and it should be entirely normal in church. Being realistic, it will be greeted variably at

---

39 https://compactmag.com/article/why-we-need-the-patriarchy (accessed November 28, 2022).

work and in the world. Yet we should keep going, and if we're glared at for holding a door, or told "I don't need you", we can simply apologise politely without getting upset. Who knows what experiences or fears lie behind an angry retort?

With all this in mind, I want to return to two very simple yet profound verses in 1 Timothy 5, which give some commonsense wisdom on how to relate to those of a different sex and age.

## CHURCH FAMILY RELATIONSHIPS: FATHERS AND BROTHERS

One of the frequent New Testament pictures for the church is that of family. Paul declares that a key reason for writing his first letter to Timothy, who is in Ephesus, is so that...

> ... you will know how people ought to conduct themselves in God's household, which is the church of the living God, the pillar and foundation of the truth. (1 Timothy 3:15)

If the world is to know the glorious truth that God is a Saviour (1:1), then the church family needs to conduct themselves in a way that ensures God's name and teaching are not slandered (3:7; 5:14; 6:1). As part of this conduct, Paul tells Timothy how he, as a younger man, is to relate to others in the church:

> Do not rebuke an older man harshly, but exhort him as if he were your father. Treat younger men as brothers, older

*women as mothers, and younger women as sisters, with absolute purity. (1 Timothy 5:1-2)*

Paul assumes that the best way for you to treat someone is going to be directed by a combination of sex, age and stage. He doesn't say, *Treat all old people like this; treat all young people like that.* Men and women are to be treated differently. To state the obvious, Paul is instructing a younger man here. If that's you, then take particular note! But there's something for all us of here, whatever our age.

The longest instruction relates to how to treat older men (possibly elders, but more likely in context to mean simply an older generation). Timothy is told not to rebuke them harshly but encourage (or exhort) them as if they were his father. It's evident that Paul thinks that younger men can be quarrelsome and take too much pleasure in arguing. In his second letter to Timothy, he writes:

*Flee the evil desires of youth and pursue righteousness, faith, love and peace ... Don't have anything to do with foolish and stupid arguments, because you know they produce quarrels. (2 Timothy 2:22-23)*

We might assume that the evil desires of youth are bound to be sexual ones, but Paul focuses upon being argumentative. Zeal needs to be combined with love (which, as we saw in the last chapter, 20-something-year-old Matt needed to be told). *So,* says Paul, *when it comes to disagreeing with an older man, treat him like your dad who has made a mistake.*

I remember hearing the scholar and preacher Don Carson talking about raising teenagers, and he said something like "I tell our kids that every rule in the house is up for negotiation and discussion, except this: I will not tolerate sass [rudeness]!" That stuck in my head—we've tried to live by that as parents, but I also think it's a good rule of thumb for younger men in churches. Feel free to question the older men about what that they believe or how they live, or anything that happens in church, but please don't be rude or rebuke harshly. We older guys are trying to model the Christian life rightly to you. If you think we're making mistakes, come and let us know, but not with a harsh rebuke. To take a very small example, there is a world of difference between commenting, "Why on earth do we have such long readings at church?" and "I'd love to have a conversation about why we tend to have long readings at church."

Of course, while Paul doesn't say this to Timothy here, he would also remind the older men in church that if they're seeking to act like fathers within their church, then they are told, "Do not exasperate your children" (Ephesians 6:4). I often think back to a couple of times when I was in my twenties and offered an opinion to older church leaders, and each time I was told, "We don't care about your opinion—we require your obedience on this issue". I can imagine that I was a bit too confident in my suggestions, but that was pretty exasperating. These weren't doctrinal issues; they were cultural applications that seemed a little outdated (like curfews on a weekend away—when I was 24! I didn't like being told to go to bed at 10:30 p.m.—although I really should be over that encounter by now.)

In fact, here in 1 Timothy, Paul doesn't tell Timothy to treat younger men as *sons* but rather to encourage or exhort them "as *brothers*" (5:1, emphasis added).[40] This may, in part, have been due to Timothy's age—he himself was clearly young (4:12). But perhaps it should give further caution to older men in churches about *demanding* obedience in small details.

A great older brother will understand what his young sibling can cope with. A 20-year-old may be up for a 15-mile hike, but a six-year-old will not be. Similarly, what you spiritually expect from a younger brother must vary, depending on his Christian "age" and maturity. Don't exasperate by demanding too much.

As children, younger brothers will tend to copy the behaviour of older siblings, so what is modelled matters. When they enter teenage years, they tend to respond better to persuasion rather than demand. If you want to encourage a brother, it helps to recognise what he will best respond to. Men in their forties and fifties will still often hold "duty" as an important value. Guys in their twenties will frequently value authenticity far more.

---

40 There is only one verb in verses 1-2: "to exhort" or "to encourage". It appears ahead of the older men and the sense carries through into the other three relationships. So it's not that we should exhort older men but not younger men.

I don't want to stray too far beyond the natural application of these verses, but I imagine that there is some application of these things beyond your church family. Younger guys: in your workplace, older men will not appreciate being rebuked harshly (including if they're junior to you in the hierarchy)—nor will they at your sports club. Older men: younger guys don't, in general, accept authority structures like I did 25 years ago (which is both good and bad)—which means that to get the best response from younger men, you'll probably need to treat them a little more like younger brothers and a little less like the "junior" who can fetch your coffee.

## MOTHERS AND SISTERS

The church family is meant to model a better pattern of living than the world can offer. It should both *model* healthy family life and be a family. The difference should be stark. The current statistics for the UK suggest that one in seven under-18s will have lived with domestic violence at some point in their childhood.[41] That is men abusing their strength against women and children in an abhorrent fashion. Young men therefore desperately need to see male strength used to serve women, to protect them, to keep them safe.

---

41 https://www.theguardian.com/commentisfree/2021/mar/14/sarah-everard-misogyny-men-violence-death-women (accessed November 28, 2022).

## Keep church safe

I'm part of a city-centre church, and so occasionally we'll get socially awkward male characters wander in. They can be slightly intimidating to young women. Most of the time they are innocent but slightly unaware that, for example, a large 50-year-old homeless guy can feel threatening to a 20-year-old woman. Very occasionally, their motives for coming in are unsavoury. So, several years ago we set up a system of BODs (Blokes on Doors) each Sunday. It's not especially sophisticated—any man large enough to possibly look like a bouncer is on a rota to stand at the door once every few weeks, alongside the other welcomers. This means that we can both care for the homeless and ensure that young women feel completely safe (and often it's younger women who are most willing to say hello and welcome such visitors to our church). It's simply men using their strength so that women feel safe. It's applying 1 Peter 3:7 beyond marriage and into the church setting:

*Husbands ... be considerate as you live with your wives, and treat them with respect as the weaker partner and as heirs with you of the gracious gift of life.*

I've realised from talking to some of the women at our church that when they're being hassled or made to feel awkward in any work or social setting, they really do want a guy to speak up. Obnoxious men will often listen to another guy in a way they will simply not to a woman.

**Show respect**

Timothy is told to encourage older women as mothers. Of course, there's a period in the teenage years when young people tend to demonstrate a lack of respect for their mothers, but, again, this tends to mature into gratitude and esteem. Paul has a delightful line in Romans 16:13: "Greet Rufus ... and his mother, who has been a mother to me, too". I take it he means that Rufus' mother had looked after him and cared for him. Consequently, he respects her, values her opinions and is thankful for her contributions.

When I preached on this little section in church, I said an unplanned line along the lines of "I don't suppose I need to say this, but guys, do expect to learn from the older women here and indeed from your younger sisters too". To my surprise, a few women afterwards thanked me and said, "You do need to say that. Sometimes men, and in particular young men, can be very patronising and dismissive."

Perhaps some of us do need reminding of how Paul speaks of his female co-workers:

*Help these women since they have contended at my side in the cause of the gospel, along with Clement and the rest of my co-workers. (Philippians 4:3)*

*Greet Tryphena and Tryphosa, those women who work hard in the Lord. Greet my dear friend Persis, another woman who has worked very hard in the Lord.*
*(Romans 16:12)*

The language of "contended at my side", "co-workers" and "worked hard in the Lord" is the same terminology Paul used of Timothy and Titus. This is how Paul treats older women and younger women—with respect.

## Love younger women as sisters

If you grew up with sisters, you'll probably have learned a lot from them. Sisters help you understand things from a female perspective. They teach you what is annoying to women and what is helpful. They give you different eyes through which to view the world. The same is true of spiritual sisters at church.

Perhaps, above all, there is a loyalty to one another among siblings. My wife and her brother rarely speak on the phone. They are very different characters. Yet in a crisis he will be one of the first to drop everything and come and help.

My sister is five years older than me. Being a churlish little brother, growing up I would often say, "I don't need another mother nagging me". As was true in many families, we knew which buttons to push if we wanted to annoy one another—but we also knew how best to comfort one another. I expect Paul is envisaging a similar development of understanding among young men and women in the church setting. Brotherly kindness means you will take the time to understand the hopes and fears of your sisters in the congregation, and brothers will be ready to drop everything to help.

I think that one positive which emerged from the horror of Sarah Everard's murder, which took place only a few miles from our church, was that men began to ask women at church about their experiences of harassment and intimidation—how common it was, when they felt unsafe, and what would help. We stopped being indifferent or unaware or just assuming that we knew. Though we didn't use the word, I think that we have learned about the sort of chivalrous behaviours that our sisters would appreciate and the sort of "mansplainy" comments that they would not.

We need to love with our words as well as our actions. One younger woman at church who discovered that I was trying to write about being a man said, "Can you tell the guys to be more gentle with 'banter'?" I asked her what she meant, and she made the observation that lots of men can be quite aggressive in their humour. Two guys who are friends can go at one another in a slightly mean way and find it genuinely funny. There's no damage done; there are no hurt feelings. Yet this same pattern often seems just mean to women. They do take it personally. They do get hurt. Lots of us may have grown up in families where siblings teased one another, but it was always in the context of family loyalty and a family-agreed level of what was acceptable. If things got out of hand, parents would intervene. As adults, we often don't have those common boundaries of acceptable humour. People come from different backgrounds. So be careful. What you think is banter may be unkind.

## Aim for absolute purity

Timothy, Paul says, is to encourage the younger women in his church as sisters "with absolute purity" (1 Timothy 5:2). He has already been told to relate to people in general "with purity" (4:12), but the reference here most likely has a sexual connotation. Most men have an instinctive "no" in their heads to objectifying their natural sisters or pondering what they might look like naked. Paul expects the same standard in relating to sisters at church—and has an application beyond it.

This precludes the use of pornography. If you're viewing porn, please don't say, "I'm not looking at sisters immorally but just at random women who have been paid to pose erotically or engage in sex online". I think you know that you're not acting as a godly protector or as a responsible man beyond reproach. You're taking. You're reducing someone down to physical appearance. You know, deep down, that's not ok. You know that this will affect the way you view other women. In a BBC survey of 18-25-year-olds, 50% of women thought that porn dehumanised women. 55% of men said that porn had been their main source of sex education.[42] If you are reading this and you are using porn, you know, really, that a godly man does not dehumanise others. Another BBC survey showed that 35% of women had suffered unwanted choking, gagging

---

42 https://www.bbc.co.uk/bbcthree/article/bb79a2ce-0de4-4965-98f0-9ebbcfcc2a60 (accessed November 28, 2022).

or slapping from a man during sex.[43] There are plenty of books to read about the negative impact of porn upon you and on how you view women. This is not going to enable you to treat young women as sisters with absolute purity. If you're not exercising self-control in this area, tell someone and do something; and confess, repent and ask for God's help to change.

Be wary also of what we could call "self-produced" porn, where we mentally undress or "enjoy" a woman we're not married to. One married friend commented to me, "My struggle is not with looking at porn—it's with looking at other women in a pure way. I can easily hear sermons warning about porn and feel good that I'm not a user. My sin is a bit more subtle." But it's still a sin, because it's not treating sisters with purity.

Most men struggle in this area. Too many of us don't talk about it, and instead excuse it or resolve each time that "That won't happen again". There is forgiveness for every sin. But there also needs to be repentance for every sin. Let me repeat: if you're struggling, don't belittle it, but equally, don't be crushed by it. Tell someone and do something.

## SO, WHAT ABOUT DATING?

For many of us, at some point a sister becomes our wife—which raises the strange-sounding question: how do I date my sister? I think that the need to encourage younger

---

43 https://comresglobal.com/wp-content/uploads/2019/11/Final-BBC-5-Live-Tables_211119cdh.pdf (accessed November 28, 2022).

women with all purity will mean that where there is any ambiguity in a male-female friendship between Christians, the man should take the initiative to clarify whether there is a possible romance or not. Take responsibility. Take the risk. If there's uncertainty, be kind and remove it.

The Bible has little explicitly to say about dating, but I define it for people as *an exclusive relationship that is exploring the potential for marriage and that grows in intimacy to a suitable degree.* (Romantic, I know!) I encourage people at our church not to make dating into too big a deal, but equally not to be unthoughtful about it. Here are three good questions to keep in mind when dating someone whom you might not marry and who might remain "just" a sister:

1. *Are we both growing as Christians?* Does she help me seek first the kingdom of God? Do I help her serve others? Do I help her commit to church?

2. *Am I honouring her—physically, emotionally and spiritually?* Until you're married, the girl you're dating may well return to being a sister, so ask: How would I treat my sister? Have we agreed what we are both comfortable with physically and what to say if one of us is not? Am I being clear where I'm at emotionally, or have I encouraged her to assume that we're closer to marriage than I think we are? If I'm ahead of her emotionally, am I going at a speed she is comfortable with?

3. *Are we making progress towards marriage?* That's not a question to ask every month, but every few months.

If the answer is no, then maybe there are good reasons to end it. It's not kind to date aimlessly while your girlfriend waits for you to propose.

If a dating relationship ends after a year or so but you can answer yes to all three questions—you both grew as Christians, you honoured her, and you made progress until the point where you realised marriage was not the right way forward—then that relationship has not "failed". It's been healthy.

It's worth underlining that one thing Paul does not say to Timothy is *Avoid women—keep them at arm's length*. He does *not* say, *Just stick with other guys; that will keep things simple and avoid the threat*. He knows that it's far healthier for men and women to relate to one another, to learn from one another, and to be encouraged by each other, keeping in mind our family relationships and therefore treating each other as mothers and fathers, brothers and sisters.

## A RETURN TO CHIVALRY

God has arranged the world so that men, in general, have more physical strength than women. A godly man uses his strength to protect and help those weaker than him. I certainly don't mean that the bigger the bicep, the godlier the man (I would not be ranked highly). I do mean that a godly man uses the strength which he has to serve others and not himself. Strength, after all, is often not purely physical. It can be relational capital; it can be "who you know" and "knowing how things happen around here". In some settings, it remains the case that men have more of this "strength" than women. Where this is the case, I think we should expect a similar mindset—a godly man uses this strength, too, to serve others rather than to be served.

That said, it is primarily physical strength that we need to think about. Just this morning a friend posted that she had been reduced to tears by a traffic warden shouting at her because her phone couldn't, for some glitchy reason, make the payment on a parking app. She wrote:

> "Men, never underestimate how intimidating it is for a 6ft-plus man to shout at a 5ft1 woman when she is on her own. I am shaking, crying and on the verge of a panic attack."

I don't suppose that guy intended to frighten her. But clearly he had forgotten that he has a physical strength that can frighten women—and, in this instance, it certainly did.

What should the Christian man have done if he'd happened to have been walking past?

He should have stepped up and stepped in. Sometimes that would be met with annoyance—often with gratitude. Always there would be a risk. But biblical masculinity looks like seeking to use the strength we have to protect and serve others, including when that carries a cost.

*Being a godly man means... showing thoughtful chivalry.*

# PRINCIPLE #6
# INVEST IN FRIENDSHIPS

*"I've been meeting with the same group of men for 36 years—here's what they've taught me."*[44]

That was the headline for a wonderful article I read recently in the *Guardian* newspaper. It was about a group of men whose commitment to one another sounded amazing. The writer, David Spiegelhalter, described how...

> *"In 1986, aged 32 and building a career as a statistician in Cambridge, I saw a notice in the local health food shop window, advertising an open meeting of a 'Men's Group'. The notice caught my eye because I was, to be honest, struggling with being a man ... I didn't have close male friends to confide in, and most of my experience of male conversation had been in the pub and consisted of opinions about 'stuff'—my work (which I enjoyed a lot), politics, sport, music, TV—often in competitive banter, each trying to better the previous story."*

---

44 https://www.theguardian.com/lifeandstyle/2022/jul/23/meeting-same-group-men-years-david-spiegelhalter (accessed November 29, 2022).

The aim of the group was "becoming a man I was proud of". Spiegelhalter goes on to describe the perceived male problems that they were trying to tackle: "loneliness, compulsive competition and lifelong emotional timidity". This group of men had clearly been enormously significant to each other. They had shared honestly the traumas of divorce, alcoholism and depression. They had shared in the joys of the wedding of one. Perhaps most movingly, when one had lost his son to cancer, the group deployed fledgling carpentry skills to make the coffin and then acted as the pallbearers.

It really was a very moving piece to read. And part of me wondered with sadness: do most men in the church have this quality of friendship?

I'm not sure we do.

## GOT MANY FRIENDS?

Surely we have the resources to do friendship really well:

- Christians know that they are saved by the grace of God and that all they have is a gift from him, so there is no need or reason for competition.

- We know that we fall short, so we can be honest about our failings.

- We know that we need others to live the Christian life, so we should naturally look to invest in friendships.

- We have the most wonderful friend in common—Jesus. He can unite men who may have nothing else in common whatsoever.

Christian men have the means to develop the very best of friendships. This chapter is simply an encouragement to do just that. Many of us will know the "body of Christ" passages of 1 Corinthians 12 or Ephesians 4. We know the "one-anothers" of the New Testament. We know in our heads that the Christian life cannot be lived alone. Yet in reality? I was struck by another newspaper headline recently:

*"Why do many middle-aged men like me have absolutely NO FRIENDS—and what toll does it take on our health?"*[45]

The author, Mark Gaisford, is the CEO of a successful business, has 40,000 connections on the professional networking website LinkedIn, and is married with two adult children. Yet he admits to being one of the 20% of men who, surveys suggest, have zero close friends. His is a well-trodden path; he has given lots of time to his family and to his career, and no time to anything else. When Christian men add in church commitments on top of our work and any family we're blessed with, our lives tend to be busy, we see lots of people, and... we can easily fail to notice that we don't actually have many friends.

---

45 https://www.dailymail.co.uk/health/article-7741723/Why-middle-aged-men-like-absolutely-NO-FRIENDS.html (accessed November 29, 2022)

You don't need to be middle-aged to lack friends—the same can be true of younger men too. It's easy to feel that you have loads of friends until you actually want to talk honestly. Social media can mask a lack of real friends because we may be "connected" to lots of people but not really have deep friendships. That is probably what lies behind the fact that in one survey 40% of British 18-24-year-olds said they felt lonely.[46] Friending people online ≠ friendship. Some of us need a nudge to get out of cyberspace and see people face to face.

Let's name some obvious reasons why we may find that our friendships are lacking (and think about what we might say about them):

- Time: This is a genuine limiting factor on friendships. But... we do always find time for the things that truly matter.

- Exhaustion: Sometimes we feel that we simply have no emotional bandwidth for anything more. That might be right. But... friendships are also emotionally refreshing and can energise us.

- Pride: We don't want to admit that we're struggling with DIY, marriage, lust or our career. We don't like to admit we're weak. But... we know that we're all failures before God!

---

46 https://www.childrenssociety.org.uk/sites/default/files/2021-01/loneliness_in_childhood.pdf (accessed November 29, 2022).

- Fear: We are scared that if we open up and are totally honest, and then the other guy doesn't and isn't, we'll look like an idiot. But... the risk of sharing honestly is well worth it.

So let's think positively. The book of Proverbs is one great place to turn to for clear thinking about the nature of friendship. It should both motivate us to pursue real friendships and equip us to do so.

## REALISM IN FRIENDSHIPS

*A man of many companions may come to ruin, but there is a friend who sticks closer than a brother.*

*(Proverbs 18:24, ESV)*

There is nothing wrong with having lots of acquaintances, but when tough times come, they will not be there. If all you have are acquaintances, you may come to "ruin"—a strong word that is used in Psalm 2 of smashing something to pieces. We can spread ourselves among a multitude of people and have no depth of heart left to give to a few. We can spend hours reading the posts of casual friends online but fail to have one friend with whom we truly share life. Quality, not quantity, is key, says Proverbs.

In their book *Friends and Friendship*, Jerry and Mary White suggest thinking in terms of four levels of friendship:

1. *Acquaintances.* These could be through work or social settings: people we enjoy meeting in an evening and

would recognise to talk to again but don't intend to pursue as friends. Some people might make as many as 500 acquaintances in a year.

2. *Casual friends.* These are people we see regularly in the normal course of life: neighbours, co-workers and perhaps relatives. We may well initiate social contact and organise to meet them. People may have somewhere between 20 and 100 casual friends.

3. *Close friends.* These are those we talk to frequently. These are friendships that endure for years, even if we move to different parts of the country or world. When we see or speak to these friends, we quickly slip back into the friendship. People tend to have between 10 and 30 close friends. (Social media can blur the boundaries between close and casual friends, as we can easily observe online where people have gone on holiday, their children's first day at school or 21st birthday, and so on, without really being close friends.)

4. *Intimate friends.* These are the people we share our lives with. We reveal to them our deepest hopes and fears, triumphs and failures. It is impossible to maintain this level of friendship with lots of people. The Whites suggest it varies between one and six intimate friends.

I've found it helpful to think through those different levels. As a pastor, I have a vast number of acquaintances through church and wider church networks. Most of these people I really like and could happily spend time with, but it's unrealistic to think that they are more than acquaintances.

I think I have a lot of casual friends too, but there have certainly been points where I have failed to notice that they are not *close* friends—and that there's a difference between these two types of friendships. My life is busy (and I think people assume it's even busier than it is), and I've had times when I've stepped back and thought, "I spend time with a lot of people, but who are my good friends?"

We all need to have at least one Christian friend who sticks closer than a brother. We need to be realistic about this— to have that quality of friendship takes time, and it takes some intentionality. I've lost track of how many times guys have said to me something like "I've given my life to work and to my family. I don't have many friends." It's never too late to change this, but it does take a deliberate decision. There are no deadlines for friendships: friends tend not to nag you like a boss who is after a piece of work or demand your attention in the same way your family does. So it's very easy for friendships to be pushed to the bottom of the to-do list and never reach the top.

I'm certainly guilty of allowing this to happen, but I've been helped enormously by some friends who are planners. I manage to get together with an old university gang three times a year, despite all of us living miles apart, because one of them puts dates in our diaries a long way ahead: the June walk, the Christmas carol service / dinner, and something in the spring. Another group of friends I know of manages a 48-hour walk most years because one guy drives it. There comes a point in life when you have to be deliberate about who you go on holiday with—if there are other couples or families where everyone gets on well, then those men are going to provide good friendships to invest in.

One other note of realism: friendships do have to begin organically. There is something to the cliché that women talk face to face while men talk shoulder to shoulder. A lot of male friendships emerge out of a common bond involving an activity. My wife can happily chat on the phone to a friend for an hour, whereas I am useless at that. I need to physically be with a friend, preferably undertaking some task (as a minimum, walking) to really feel relaxed in the conversation. As a man, I don't think I'm unusual in that.

Over time, the task or activity becomes slightly less important. If you've spent enough time with someone and shared the ups and downs of your life, then friendship will have emerged. As one guy at church in his early thirties said to me. "I've been here a decade, and a lot of the people I first clicked naturally with have now left the city. So, I look around at my peers and think, 'Ok, it's us—and so you're my mates. I didn't have you as my first picks, but we've now done a lot of life together, and I've grown to love your friendship and company.'"

That's realism and wisdom. Proximity really matters to friendships, and so while you may have great friends on the end of a phone, you also need friends whom you can see at the end of the day. A weekend in the countryside with rarely seen friends cannot replace every week in church with people who see the ebb and flow of your life.

## THE BENEFITS OF FRIENDSHIP

Writing about friendship, C.S. Lewis observed:

> "Friendship is unnecessary, like philosophy, like art, like the universe itself (for God did not need to create). It has no survival value; rather it is one of those things which give value to survival."[47]

That's true. Yet I would suggest that the Bible promotes friendship as even more important than that. It doesn't merely add value; it's essential for healthy Christian living. In this sense, it's a necessity.

### Handling hardship

Friends who turn up when you need them are very precious:

> Many claim to have unfailing love, but a faithful person who can find? (Proverbs 20:6)

> Like a broken tooth or a lame foot is reliance on the unfaithful in a time of trouble. (25:19)

---

47 C.S. Lewis, *The Four Loves* (William Collins, 2015), p 71.

Science was never my strongest suit at school, but I understand simple equations:

hardship + friendship = maturity

hardship + loneliness = destructive sin

Life is tricky, and we need friends to help us get through. Going through tough times alone can easily lead us into destructive sinful behaviour. But friends who will listen to us, grieve with us and sit with us make an enormous difference. They can remind us of truth that we may know but still need to hear again.

One of the great examples in Scripture is found in 1 Samuel 23. David is on the run for his life because King Saul views him as a threat to his reign. Yet Jonathan, the king's son, tracks him down:

> *Jonathan went to David at Horesh and helped him to find strength in God. (1 Samuel 23:16)*

That's a wonderful phrase: he "helped him to find strength in God". One of the men who understand this best was the 20th-century German pastor Dietrich Bonhoeffer. He told his students at their illegal seminary during the Second World War:

> *"The Christian needs another Christian who speaks God's word to him. He needs him again and again as he becomes uncertain and discouraged ... He needs his brother solely because of Jesus Christ. The Christ in his own heart is*

*weaker than the Christ in the word of his brother."*[48]

Bonhoeffer is saying that sometimes familiar truths that we already know come with a renewed power when someone says them to us. We may know biblical truth about Jesus, but we still need to hear it from a friend.

My thoughts drift to the periods when I have most needed another Christian to speak to me. There was the time when my wife was in hospital for several months, and the friends who visited her also took me out to see how I was going. I'm grateful for the wisdom of Seb, who would drag me off for a drink, ignore what was going on in the hospital, and tell me inane stories until I laughed. It was a wonderful tonic.

Then there was the time we suffered a crushing bereavement, and one friend, Jod, decided to finish work, drive for three hours, sit with me for an hour, and then drive for three hours home to be at work the next day. He could have phoned, but he knew that physical presence brings a different level of comfort. I think of Mike, who sat with me for hours in the pub around the same time. I think of Andy and the multiple times when he has dropped his work to come and lift me up in family crises.

Sometimes we need our friends to be there with us and for us, to tell us what we know is true and to keep us going.

---

48 Dietrich Bonhoeffer, *Life Together*, (Harper and Brothers, 1954), p 25.

## GROWING IN CHARACTER

Who you choose as your friends will make a difference to who you become:

> *Whoever walks with the wise becomes wise, but the companion of fools will suffer harm.*
>
> *(Proverbs 13:20, ESV)*

If you want to be wise, choose wise friends. If you want to be godly, choose godly friends. If you want to be obsessed with money, choose worldly friends. If you want to become a moaner, choose cynical friends. We do, to a large extent, get to choose who we walk with. Our friends will shape our character.

We know this. Most parents will have thought on occasions, "I don't think he/she is a good influence on my son/daughter". But are we as thoughtful about how we are being influenced by friends?

> *As iron sharpens iron, so one man sharpens another.*
> *(Proverbs 27:17, NIV84)*

Here is a picture from the forge: a slightly forceful image of being bashed into shape. Good friendship will contain the occasional rebuke but also provide encouragement:

> *Perfume and incense bring joy to the heart, and the pleasantness of a friend springs from their heartfelt advice. (Proverbs 27:9)*

These are the words from a friend that are like a beautiful scent, that lift you up and make life better—and make *you* better. As a pastor, I go to plenty of weddings and hear lots of wedding speeches. Undoubtedly one of the nicest comments I heard in a best-man's speech was a few years back:

*"Thank you for having me as your best man. Thank you much more for making me a better man."*

What a great testimony of a great friendship. Over time, this friendship had helped the best man to grow in character. It made me think, "Who has done that for me?"—then, having called them to mind, I made sure I thanked them.

Having friends like that entails having friends who can speak candidly:

*Better is open rebuke than hidden love. Wounds from a friend can be trusted, but an enemy multiplies kisses.*
*(Proverbs 27:5)*

*Whoever flatters his neighbour is spreading a net for his feet. (Proverbs 29:5, NIV84)*

Over the years I've had plenty of wounds from people who were not friends and were not kind in how they rebuked me. Yet I can also vividly remember certain conversations when a friend was kind enough to gently wound me. I think of Hugh rebuking me after an elders' meeting for being too angry; Richard doing so after a conference for being too confident of my opinions; Andy doing so (on more than one occasion) for being too gloomy; Phil doing so in one season for being too abrupt with people; Mike doing so for being too slow to offer forgiveness to someone who had wronged me; Marc doing so for not listening to advice. They were all right! (Brothers, if you are reading this, thank you; you changed me for the better with your rebukes!). And these are just the ones I instantly remember.

Sometimes you need friends who will tell you that you've got something wrong and that you need to change. A real friend is one who loves you enough to risk your annoyance in order to tell you what you need to hear.

## HOW TO BE A GOOD FRIEND

My great encouragement to you is simply this: invest deeply in a few friendships. There may only be three or four friends that you take with you for the whole of your adult life. There may be some who are wonderful friends for a few years but then circumstances intervene and the relationship tails off. That's ok; it happens, but then go again, because we all need some friends who we see regularly. Here are three things it would be great to do:

### 1. Invest

You have to commit to friendship. Sometimes it costs money to go on holiday with someone or to spend a night camping with a mate. It always costs time (and if you have a family, be sure you reciprocate their enabling of this by taking care of everything so that your wife can go away with friends). But the pay-off is definitely worthwhile.

I asked a dear friend—who I've known for 30 years and who was my best man—why it was that we were such good friends when actually we're really quite different. We have different temperaments, different hobbies and families of very different ages. We've had years living in different countries from each other (although I was better on the phone in those days, and we did travel to meet up). He summarised it well: "Our friendship is intentional and spiritual". We have been very deliberate about seeing one another, and we have spoken about Jesus and our lives following him. We've invested in one another.

I've met with the same two other guys to pray together for many years. It happens once a month (mostly) because we get up early and meet before work. I'm never thrilled when the alarm clock shrills early, but I am incredibly grateful for the friendships that have emerged over the years. I certainly wouldn't want to reclaim the time for anything else. In one sense, we don't have the time to meet regularly; so we *make* the time to do so.

## 2. Be honest

I had a funny conversation with someone at church recently. I'll call him Jim.

*Me:* Have you got a time when we could meet up in the next couple of weeks?

*Jim:* Sure. What is it you want to talk about? What's on your agenda?

*Me:* Erm, I don't know. I just wanted to hang out and catch up.

Despite knowing each other for many years, I realised that we had slipped into only talking about church business and issues and that therefore our friendship had stagnated a little. I did feel a bit silly saying to a 50-year-old man, "I just want to hang out as a friend". Yet he was delighted. I guess there aren't too many guys who think, "Actually, I've already got too many good friends that I can share life deeply with".

Real friendships require honesty. In that Mark Gaisford article that asked why so many middle-aged men have "absolutely NO FRIENDS", there's one very telling paragraph:

> "I joined a local meet-up group for people looking to make friends, and arranged to meet a man of my age for a drink. But I was plagued with worries—what do we talk about? Can I mention feeling lonely? How honest is too honest? In the end, we chatted about the weather for 20 minutes, then went our separate ways. Neither of us wanted to go any deeper, for fear of compromising our manliness."

It's a little ironic that in a national newspaper he can be honest about his inability to be honest! Christian men must do better than this. I have one friend to whom, when we meet up, I now will say at some point, "Come on then, confess your sins to me". That's in a friendship of a couple of decades, and so I'm content that it's appropriate to say it so bluntly, but we have to start somewhere with this. Generally in our churches and in our Christian friendships, when we talk about our triumphs it can create competition; when we talk about our failures it builds community. That's true for friendships too. You'll never have great friendships unless you can be honest. Make a start and grow in this.

## 3. Forgive

The greatest friend you could have will still not be Jesus! They're flawed (like you) and will get it wrong (like you). If you wait for the perfect friend, then you'll be lonely. If a mate annoys you and in your irritation you let a lot of time pass, then the friendship might just fizzle out. I was helped in this years ago by an old hymn of John Newton's:

*One there is, above all others,*
*Well deserves the name of friend;*
*His is love beyond a brother's,*
*Costly, free, and knows no end.*

*Could we bear from one another*
*What he daily bears from us?*
*Yet this glorious friend and brother*
*Loves us though we treat him thus.*

Jesus forgives, and so can we.

## INVEST IN FRIENDS

Friendships give value to life. More than that, they shape and determine who we are. To put it bluntly, one day you will stop work, and your colleagues will forget you. One day parents will die, and children will leave home, and your phone will ring less. Who are the friends you will spend your time with? As men, it is easy to relegate this rich blessing of friendship to the bottom of our mental task list. That's foolish. Only when the storms come and there's no friend to turn to do we realise how important friends are.

So, for the sake of your health and the health of your Christian life, be a godly man by investing in his friendships. Don't lament that currently you don't have the friendships you desire—go out and be a good friend to one or two guys. You may well find that they respond in kind and a casual friendship becomes a far deeper one. As someone commented to me recently, "My grandfather always said, 'To have a friend, you have to be a friend.' I think he was right."

*Being a godly man means... investing in some real friendships.*

# PRINCIPLE #7
# RAISE HEALTHY "SONS"

For most men, the most significant influence on their understanding of manhood is their dad—for better or for worse.

For some of us, the absence of a father, literally or emotionally, has had a large impact. Some men will have painful memories of how their father treated them and what they learned of "being a man" from him. Personally, I'm very thankful that my dad gave me a largely positive role model. One of my earliest memories of Christmas Days is going with him to take presents to people at the local geriatric hospital before we could open most of our own ("Why, Dad?" "Because it is kind, and it's no good being self-absorbed."). He always encouraged me to ask neighbours if they needed any help with gardening or decorating ("Why, Dad?" "Because money has to be earned."). He told me, aged 11, to take on a paper round to deliver newspapers even though I was too small to carry the large sack of papers ("Why, Dad?" "Because hard work is good for you."). Yet he would accompany me on the paper round to carry the load (because, alongside these other lessons, he wanted me to know that he loved me). He wasn't perfect, of course, but he was fairly consistent, and he was there when I needed him. I'm very thankful for him.

Fathering matters. It makes a difference. And one final element of being a godly man is to aim to raise godly "sons". I use quotation marks because we've already seen that single men, such as the apostle Paul, had a crucial role as a father figure in the lives of younger men:

> But you know that Timothy has proved himself, because as a son with his father he has served with me in the work of the gospel. (Philippians 2:22)

> I appeal to you for my child, Onesimus, whose father I became in my imprisonment. (Philemon v 10, ESV)

> In Christ Jesus I became your father through the gospel.
> (1 Corinthians 4:15)[49]

So, although we'll begin by looking at fathers in the home, please don't skip this chapter if you're not a biological or adoptive dad. You still have an enormously valuable role to play in modelling the faith to younger boys and men. Much of what we'll say about fathers in the home has echoes in how you can mentor younger men.

---

49 Here it is not an individual that Paul refers to but a whole church. Nevertheless it is striking that, as a single man, Paul still reached for the language of fatherhood to demonstrate how he cared for them.

## FATHERS IN THE HOME: TRAIN AND INSTRUCT

If you're a dad, you know that parenting is a wonderful privilege and a massive challenge. Some guys do just seem to have delightful kids and can perhaps think, "What's so hard about being a dad?" But not everything is down to nurture; some things come from a given nature. As one friend observed to me, "If we had only had two children, we'd be pretty arrogant parents, as they are both diligent, self-motivated, polite kids. Fortunately, we had a third child, and while we love her, wow, she has been a challenge and the source of many tears. She has made us have a lot more sympathy for other parents." (In my view, she's pretty great too, but hey, I'm not her parents!) So, first lesson: be kind when you look at other dads and how they're doing.

The Bible assumes that the normal structure of a family has the father as its head—indeed, the Greek word for family is derived from father.[50] So when Paul addresses Christian households in Ephesians 6, he tells the dads:

*Fathers, do not exasperate your children; instead, bring them up in the training and instruction of the Lord. (6:4)*

To take the positives first: dads are to bring their kids up (or nourish them) in, first, the "training ... of the Lord". The word "training" has the sense of preparing a

---

50 "For this reason I kneel before the Father [*pater*], from whom every family [*patria*] in heaven and on earth derives its name." (Ephesians 3:14-15)

child for life, in morals and wisdom through education and chastisement.[51] Paul is telling fathers that they are responsible for shaping their kids' values and priorities to be godly ("in the Lord"). Fundamentally this means teaching them the gospel, but it also has the wider sense of ensuring that children are ready for life—of teaching the next generation of children how to budget, how to make decisions, how to serve, and so on.

My son is due to leave home for university in a few months' time. I asked him if there was anything he wanted from me to help prepare him for life away from our home. His answer was "I suppose I should know how to iron, and it would be good to be able to cook more than spaghetti bolognese". To be honest, I was looking for something more profound than that. Have I prepared him to handle peer pressure? Is he clear on the priority of settling quickly at a good church? Time will tell. But my job was to help prepare him for life. If you have a son, he needs you to equip him not to need you.

---

51 Here is the Websters Lexicon for the Greek word translated "training" in Ephesians 6:4:

1. The whole training and education of children (which relates to the cultivation of mind and morals, and employs for this purpose now commands and admonitions, now reproof and punishment). It also includes the training and care of the body and 2. whatever in adults also cultivates the soul, esp. by correcting mistakes and curbing passions.

a) instruction which aims at increasing virtue

b) chastisement, chastening, (of the evils with which God visits men for their amendment)

Part of training is discipline. Boys do need boundaries, and it's kind to provide them. I've yet to see a tennis match where the players complain that someone has painted lines on the ground. No lines = chaos and frustration. Clear lines = a fun and competitive game with agreed rules.

In an instruction that the New Testament repeats (Hebrews 12:5-6), the writer of Proverbs writes:

> *My son, do not despise the LORD's discipline, and do not resent his rebuke, because the LORD disciplines those he loves, as a father the son he delights in.*
>
> *(Proverbs 3:11-12)*

It's well over 20 years since I was a schoolteacher, but there are certain conversations I will never forget. One was when sitting with a talented 18-year-old boy in his final year of school and his successful, busy, affluent parents. The boy was going to flunk his final school exams, and so we'd called the parents in to try and formulate a plan. It emerged that they had given him a lot of money and freedom to go out and party, and not a lot of parameters. At one telling point in the conversation, the boy shouted:

> *"I wish you loved me enough to ground me!"*

It was an awkward moment. Here was one young man who could see that a part of parental love is kind discipline. We live in a culture where sometimes parents are scared to discipline their kids because they overly desire their children's friendship. We need to remember that it's impossible to prepare boys (or girls) for life without exercising appropriate discipline.

Of course, the pendulum can swing too far the other way. We are talking about loving discipline, not bullying or harshness in a parent. If you are frequently shouting at your kids at full volume, that's a red flag. If you frequently belittle your kids, that's a red flag. They are children lacking maturity—we should expect them to make mistakes and help them grow, and not crush them mercilessly so as to break their spirit. If you're a dad, it's worth asking yourself which way you lean (currently)— towards a lack of discipline or towards harshness. We should not be overly concerned about whether our kids want to hang out with us, nor should we desire to beat them into submission. We're fathers, seeking to bring them up to know the Lord and prepare them for life. Let the living God be your model.

Second, the "instruction of the Lord" appears to be a slightly narrower term, relating to exhortation. Put simply, fathers are to teach their kids about Jesus and urge them to follow him. Most family devotion times are chaotic and unsatisfactory. But ask adult Christians what they can remember of family devotions and the common response is "Not a lot, but we always did them". That says a huge amount! Occasionally someone might recall, "We prayed for the persecuted church every night" or "Dad was obsessed with praying for Romania". Kids will not remember much of the detail, but they will remember what was important to you, and whether that included opening the Bible with them.

## DON'T EXASPERATE

The negative command in Ephesians 6:4 is quite simple (to understand, not necessarily to obey): "Do not exasperate your children" (NIV) or "Do not provoke [them] to anger" (ESV).

What might this look like? I'm sure that dads have invented numerous and varied ways to exasperate their children—but I wonder if one of the most commons lines we hear from our sons is "You don't listen to me". Now, that may be unfair. It may simply mean that they've asked for more sweets / pocket money / a later curfew; you did listen but they didn't get what they wanted. However, it's a line that needs to be evaluated when we hear it. Is it true?

This is especially relevant in the later teen years as kids move into adulthood and everyone is navigating that tricky period when they move towards greater independence. I've found it hard in the past that my son can be rude to me in a way that I would never have dreamed of being to my own father. Yet, in part, I've come to see that in a culture which has moved to greater informality and less inherent respect for authority, I really shouldn't take it so personally. Wisdom is knowing the right time to pick your battles!

In the same conversation with my son as when I asked what help he needed to prepare for leaving home, I steeled myself and asked him what were the most frequent ways that I exasperated him. I'll spare you the details as I don't want to double the length of this chapter, but it was actually a very helpful conversation. It wasn't just one-way traffic—he was able to see why I acted in certain ways and even begrudgingly see that, just occasionally, I might have a point.

Again, we need to pick our moments! Many teenagers have body clocks that mean they are at their most willing to talk about things just at the moment when you want to go to bed. But calm feedback can be very useful. Even from a teenage son.

Another common way in which we as dads can exasperate our sons is in expecting them to conform to our values, preferences and goals in too many things. Some dads seem to want to raise a "mini me"—a little clone of themselves. All fathers should long for their sons to follow Christ and serve him wholeheartedly. But after that, nothing matters very much. If they are nothing like you (other than in the ways you are like Jesus), then that's fine.

I think my own father modelled this very well. He was an excellent sportsman—he played county cricket—and I was not. He was a brilliant handyman, able to fix anything at home—repair pipes, restore broken furniture, mend faulty electrics—and I could just about wire a plug. In his late seventies he was still physically stronger than me. Yet he let me develop differently and took pleasure in the things I enjoyed. He'd left school aged 15 and never really read more than a newspaper article, but he read everything I wrote and told me how proud he was. He'd listen to my sermons and ask me how on earth I could talk like that.

Now that I'm the father of a young man with very different gifts, skills and ambitions to mine, I realise that my dad must have found it harder than I realised when his son was a DIY dunce and a cricketing calamity. But I don't think I knew at the time.

Along the same lines, some fathers can exasperate their children by expecting them to fulfil dreams that they had but never fulfilled. Perhaps, the subconscious logic goes, life has turned out to be a little disappointing, but... there is a second chance of success through my son. Might it be that this lies behind the dads who scream at their kids on the sides of sports pitches, berating them for every little mistake and treating every game as though it's vital to their future happiness?

More subtle but related to this is the temptation to try and win praise for yourself through your children. Someone confessed to me recently that they had realised they were harsher on their kids when they were playing after church than they were when they were playing at home. In his words, "I wanted to look like a Good Christian Dad at church in front of others, so I 'needed' the kids to behave super-well at church". It took a friend to notice and point it out to him.

Sometimes, we need reminding that we are just stewarding our sons for a little while. We are to help shepherd them to maturity. We are to keep pointing them to Jesus and then let them be their own man.

## FATHERS IN THE FAITH

Every man can be a father in the faith to a younger man. In the modern world in which, from the age of 18, many boys will not regularly see their fathers, it's a priceless role. In our church there are plenty of young men who are thrilled when an older guy takes an interest in them and offers to mentor them. You could be that guy.

Don't say, "I couldn't do that". Don't set the bar too high. No one realistically expects perfection; they hope to see progress (1 Timothy 4:15). Help a younger guy to see biblically what it means to be male, tell them what you've learned about getting it right and wrong, and be there for them when they need prayer or advice.

This is not a replacement for a biological father; often, it's a complement to the ongoing work of dads. However, there are young men who, for whatever reason, have no dad (or no dad who they know), and those guys *really* need you. Since 2000, in the UK a quarter of all children have grown up in single-parent families. (In Australia the figure is 14%, and in the US it is 30%.)[52] There are a lot

---

52 The numbers are hard to compare across nations, but see:
www.theguardian.com/education/2022/sep/01/next-pm-urged-to-put-families-at-the-heart-of-policymaking-plans

of boys who are lacking a father and who need Christian men to be that for them. Otherwise, what are the voices that will shape them? Guys who never saw their father being present, loving, firm and kind are likely to repeat those mistakes in the next generation. A spiritual father can break that cycle.

Some dads would love to be there for their kids, but cannot be. Jonathan Tjarks was a Christian sports journalist who died from cancer, aged 35, in September 2022. He wrote an exceptionally moving piece shortly before dying, titled, "Does my son *know* you?" He described how he struggled with the fact that *his* father was diagnosed with Parkinson's disease when he was twelve, and therefore "although he was there, he was no longer *there*". Above all else, Tjarks wanted to be there for his son, but he knew that he was about to die when his own son was only two years old. In a striking line he wrote:

*"I have already told some of my friends: When I see you in heaven, there's only one thing I'm going to ask—Were you good to my son and my wife? Were you there for them? Does my son **know** you?"*[53]

All of us can be spiritual fathers to sons in the faith.

www.abs.gov.au/statistics/labour/employment-and-unemployment/labour-force-status-families/latest-release

census.gov/library/stories/2021/04/number-of-children-living-only-with-their-mothers-has-doubled-in-past-50-years.html (all accessed November 29, 2022).

53 https://www.theringer.com/2022/3/3/22956353/fatherhood-cancer-jonathan-tjarks (accessed November 29, 2022).

You can start this young, by teaching younger boys in Sunday school. I love the fact that so many young men help to run the children's Sunday school at our church. They are priceless role models, and I have to remember to remind them that they are not merely teaching young ones the content of the Christian faith; they are modelling what it looks like to live it out. That, of course, includes serving others.

I enjoy the story of the youthful Teddy Roosevelt, long before he became US President, helping to teach Sunday School when a young man. One day, ten-year-old Tom entered the class with a black eye. Roosevelt asked him, "What happened?" Tom replied, "An older kid was picking up on my sister so I hit him. He then hit me back." Roosevelt's response was "Well done, Tom"—for which he was sacked from his role.[54] But Roosevelt was right to applaud the noble instinct in Tom that wanted to use the strength he had to protect his sister. He was teaching Tom that avoidance and cowardice is not the right way to live as a man. (And, yes, they could probably have talked further about approaches to bullying that did not involve swinging first...)

When boys are in their late teens and are developing more independence, an "older brother" figure who is less than a decade older can be an enormous blessing. It's quite possible that a teenager will have deeper (or different)

---

54 Paul F. Boller "Theodore Roosevelt" in *Presidential Anecdotes* (Oxford University Press, 1981), p 201.

spiritual conversations with someone who is an "older peer", a few steps further on than them, than they will with their "old" dad. If you're that dad, don't worry; it's normally only for a season. If you could be that kind of "older brother", you can make an enormous difference (and one day, if you become an old dad, you'll understand just how grateful that guy's father was).

## WE NEED TO TALK ABOUT SEX

Back to fathering your own children... We need, before we end this chapter, to dwell upon one specific area where boys need help in the "training of the Lord": growing up in a hypersexualised culture. We should not be leaving these conversations to our wives. This *is* hard and awkward—first, because the online world of pornography is one that many of us never experienced or had to navigate at that age; and secondly, because it's, well, awkward to talk about.

But we must.

I read a lot of newspaper articles in the past year with headlines such as...

*"Porn obsessed or confused? The trouble with being a teenage boy today."*[55]

*"My 13-year-old son is being exposed to porn—how can I protect him?"*[56]

55 Alice Thomson, *The Times*, Saturday June 5, 2021.

56 https://www.theguardian.com/lifeandstyle/2022/may/27/my-13-year-old-

We need to have had a conversation with boys about online pornography by the age of eleven. The most recent authoritative survey in the UK, by the British Board of Film Classification, found that 51% of 11-13-year-olds reported seeing online porn, rising to 66% of 14-15-year olds.[57] Some children report seeing it as young as aged seven or eight. In contrast, 75% of parents of 15-year-olds thought that their children hadn't watched porn online. That's a big mismatch. The content is awful—one in eight first-time viewers saw acts of sexual violence, rape and other non-consensual acts.

I'm sorry. I hate writing this as much as I imagine you hate reading it. We want to live in denial, but that doesn't help our boys. We have to talk about it.

In my limited experience, it's actually easier when boys are a little younger; they are less receptive in the teen years. Dads must take a view on when they want to introduce the topic, but sometimes the news makes it easier. When the *Everyone's Invited* website became big news in the UK, it was quite easy to talk to my son about what he and his friends thought about misogyny or banter and about what healthy relationships with girls look like. Every so often the porn industry and its crazy profits will make the news; maybe that's the time to check your son's understanding of how far from real life

son-is-being-exposed-to-porn-how-can-i-protect-him (accessed November 29, 2022).

57 Quoted in *The Week*, April 24, 2021.

these sites are, and how damaging and addictive they are. If it proves impossible to have this kind of conversation, that, again, is where a (carefully chosen) "big brother" at church can prove to be a great blessing.

Of course, this is only one facet of Christian discipleship. If your son has developed the confidence to express different beliefs from his peers about Jesus, then he'll be able to express different views in regard to sexual ethics too. It's a larger part of helping our boys grow in expressing their views graciously but confidently.

## MODEL THE GOSPEL AND ENJOY THE RIDE

There comes a point in every boy's life when they realise their dad is fallible—a moment when, as fathers, we go from being a hero to a bit of a disappointment.

I remember being with one friend whose son told him:

> *"Daddy, you know my best friend at school; his dad was the England Rugby Captain."*
>
> *"Yes, I know."*
>
> *"Dad, did you ever play rugby for England?"*
>
> *"No, son."*
>
> *"Oh…"*

And just like that, his dad had lost his superhero status.

More significantly, there comes a point when every boy realises that their dad is morally fallible. They can see that their dad has got it wrong—in an angry argument with someone else, in being unfair at home or in being harsh towards them.

While remembering that, as a parent, we have authority and are to be setting boundaries, we also need to model the fact that we are sinners who need forgiveness. You need to be ready to apologise to your kids and admit when you have got things wrong—to be willing to say, "I'm sorry. I got that wrong. Please will you forgive me?"

I've been particularly struck that boys whose dads are pastors can often remember the first time their dad sat down and actually said to them, "I got that wrong". That hits me hard because I'm a pastor myself, and a pastor is meant to model repentance. But every Christian dad needs to model to their children that the Christian life is not one merely or primarily of moral conformity—it is a life of repentance and faith. It's a life in which behaviour flows out of knowing that God accepts us, not out of a desire to achieve acceptance.

Of course, there's a wisdom call in how young you start doing this. It's not very helpful to ask a two-year-old for forgiveness—that's just confusing. But there are appropriate ways of doing this in a child's primary-school years; and certainly with teenagers, in that stage when they are developing their own views and pushing boundaries, we need to model being forgiven sinners who need the grace of Jesus. Don't model Pharisee-like behaviour, insisting on standards for your children and then excusing or ignoring your own failure to match them. It's Jesus, above all, who we want our children to love; and it's repentance, not pretending we're good, that is the way we enter into and then enjoy a relationship with him.

One last thing: enjoy the privilege of being a father— whether it's fathering your own children, fathering in the faith, or both. It's a role that causes stress, pain and tears, but also great joys. None of us are as good at it as we would desire. But that's ok. All of us can get better. We should try our best to be beyond reproach, but we can only ever parent by grace. If we model following Jesus to the next generation, we have served that generation, and we have served Jesus.

Stop for a moment and reflect on what this could look like for you. What do you want to do differently, in your home and/or in your church?

*Being a godly man means... seeking to raise healthy "sons".*

# CONCLUSION: PROGRESS

We began by saying that we needed something positive to say about men rather than just blaming them. Just this morning I read of some research from Kings College, London under the headline:

*Why stressed dads might be to blame for their rowdy child's terrible twos*[58]

There we go... another thing that guys are to blame for! Hopefully, in this book we've made progress towards reclaiming masculinity—not by returning to flawed models of the past nor by asserting our own cultural preferences but by looking to the Bible. Although each part needs some thoughtful working out in your own life, the seven biblical principles we've seen are that a godly man...

1. recognises that men and women are different but doesn't exaggerate this.

---

58 https://www.telegraph.co.uk/news/2022/10/11/why-stressed-dads-might-blame-rowdy-childs-terrible-twos/ (accessed November 29, 2022).

2. takes responsibility to provide sacrificial leadership in a fashion appropriate to the roles and relationships that he is in.

3. is ambitious for the kingdom of God.

4. uses his strength to fight to protect God's church.

5. shows thoughtful chivalry by offering his strength to serve others.

6. invests in his friendships.

7. seeks to raise spiritually healthy "sons".

You might have noticed that this is not really completing the sentence "Being a godly man means…"—it's more the creation of seven sentences! So we can boil all of these down to something like this:

*Being a godly man means taking responsibility to lead, being ambitious for God's kingdom, using your strength to protect the church and serve others, investing in friends, and raising "sons".*

Hopefully, I've not broken the promises that I made to you in the introduction. I have tried not to irritate you either by being overly prescriptive or by failing to state what I think each principle looks like in practice. I certainly have tried not to beat you up. Yet it's quite easy to get to the end of this sort of book with lots of new resolutions, but then think, "I don't know where to start". Good intentions can easily be thwarted by the chaos of life. And in that atmosphere, and aware of our own flaws, it's easy to drift into thinking, "I knew I was failing as a man, and now I've got seven ways to define my failures..."

Please don't be crushed. Instead, resolve (preferably with a friend) to make progress.

That's what the Lord loves to see in us. He's a good Father, who is incredibly patient with our shortcomings. He doesn't expect perfection in you or me. He does love to see progress.

There is something wonderfully reassuring in Paul's words to his spiritual son, Timothy:

> Don't let anyone look down on you because you are young, but set an example for the believers in speech, in conduct, in love, in faith and in purity. Until I come, devote yourself to the public reading of Scripture, to preaching and to teaching. Do not neglect your gift, which was given you through prophecy when the body of elders laid their hands on you.
>
> Be diligent in these matters; give yourself wholly to them, so that everyone may see your progress. Watch your life and doctrine closely. Persevere in them, because if you do, you will save both yourself and your hearers.
>
> (1 Timothy 4:12-16)

Timothy has been given a daunting task by Paul—to sort out the church in Ephesus by rebuking false teachers and by changing the conduct of the church family so that the message of God as Saviour is clearly heard. And Timothy is told to "set an example for the believers in speech, in conduct, in love, in faith and in purity".

How does he start on all that?

*Be diligent in these matters … so that everyone may see your progress.*

I think that progress is achievable for all of us. It may be dramatic, or it may be slow. A couple of weeks ago, I was asked publicly at church if I could recall a time when I had made really rapid progress in godliness and, if so, what had made the difference. I stood silent for a while before replying, "In all honesty, I don't think I've ever made very rapid progress in godliness. It's been slow progress, month on month, year on year. But I know that there's been progress over time. Others encourage me that they've seen it too."

So, as you finish this book, please don't despair. Just try to be a better man today than you were yesterday. (Or, perhaps more realistically, a better man this year than you were last year.) Pray to that end. On some days you'll be conscious you've "won"; on others you might "lose"— but it's the progress made over a year that matters. But at the same time, be deliberate rather than vague. 1 Timothy 4:15 reminds us that we're unlikely to make progress unless we resolve to be *diligent* in pursuing it. It doesn't happen by accident. You need to be intentional in your choices and deliberate in pursuing Christ-likeness, and then let God's Spirit do his work. So meet up with another man or two and make resolutions together—realistic ones, involving achievable changes—and then pray for one another and encourage one another.

Be realistic about your personality and circumstances. Don't decide you're going to undertake a Masters in Theology to better nourish your family if you're in full-time work with three kids under five years old. Lots of what we have looked at under these seven principles of masculinity is not seen in grand sweeping changes but in your small daily decisions and interactions. Pray that you would make progress in those.

And, when you know you have messed up (and it will happen), look at Jesus. He is the perfect man, who chose to die for you. When he died, he took your failings and nailed them to the cross (Colossians 2:14), so that you can always be forgiven and so that there is mercy for you every day. He does not only show you how to be a man (though he does); in his death, he declares that you can be forgiven for every failing in how you live as a man. He is not surprised when you mess up; he knew you would, and he has already died to take the punishment for it, and he rose again to send his Spirit to live in you to enable you to change.

So don't give up on the basis that you haven't achieved perfection and never will this side of heaven. Acknowledge that you need forgiveness, be assured that because of the cross you have forgiveness, and retain your ambition to make progress, with the Lord's help, over a few months or a few years. Remember, God is a patient Father. He longs for you to make progress, but he also extends you mercy and grace. He is gracious and compassionate, slow to anger and rich in love.

We'll finish with one "traditionally manly" story. Years ago, when training for ministry, I did a placement as a chaplain at the Royal Military Academy in Sandhurst, where the British Army trains its officers. One day, all the officer cadets slunk into the main lecture hall. It was rarely electric when the whole college of 700 cadets plus staff was addressed. But that day the visiting speaker was a general who was a Christian, and his message was essentially this:

> "Let me ask you, what will keep you on the battlefield when bullets are flying past your head?
>
> "You all think you'll stand by your men. Not all will. I've seen officers throw down their guns and run; I've seen officers hide in a hole and wait until the firefight was over. Only if you are rooted in something more substantial than yourself will you stand and fight. For myself, I'm rooted in Jesus Christ. He gives me strength to fight when I would rather run. I believe that you have to find something greater than yourself to root your life in if you are to be a useful officer. I recommend you root yourself in Jesus Christ."

His talk caused outrage, but it certainly gave me useful conversations for the next week!

We all fail at being godly men. None of us are the guys we long to be or exactly who God wants us to be. But there is always forgiveness for that. And so we can make progress, and we will make progress, if we remain rooted in Jesus Christ. He is greater than you, and he will strengthen you. So, have a go. Be a better man today than you were yesterday.

So I invite you to join with me (a stumbling, often failing guy) in seeking to live as a godly man—to reclaim masculinity from the flaws of the past and the confusion of the present. We can, with our brothers, live out a masculinity that we are proud of and others are thankful for. Jesus thinks we can do this. We won't do it perfectly— but we can make progress.

# ACKNOWLEDGEMENTS

Thank you to all those who read through an early draft of the manuscript and suggested improvements. You really did make it significantly better. Thanks to Rufus, Jonell, Liz, Neil, Will, Helen and Amy.

Thanks again to Carl for persuading me that this was a good idea and then for your gracious editing. It's a pleasure, sir.

Finally, thanks to Nathan for enduring so many of my mistakes over the years and still believing I was qualified to write this. I love you, son.

**the good book**
C O M P A N Y

**BIBLICAL | RELEVANT | ACCESSIBLE**

At The Good Book Company, we are dedicated to helping Christians and local churches grow. We believe that God's growth process always starts with hearing clearly what he has said to us through his timeless word—the Bible.

Ever since we opened our doors in 1991, we have been striving to produce Bible-based resources that bring glory to God. We have grown to become an international provider of user-friendly resources to the Christian community, with believers of all backgrounds and denominations using our books, Bible studies, devotionals, evangelistic resources, and DVD-based courses.

We want to equip ordinary Christians to live for Christ day by day, and churches to grow in their knowledge of God, their love for one another, and the effectiveness of their outreach.

Call us for a discussion of your needs or visit one of our local websites for more information on the resources and services we provide.

Your friends at The Good Book Company

thegoodbook.com | thegoodbook.co.uk
thegoodbook.com.au | thegoodbook.co.nz
thegoodbook.co.in